THE VOICE OF
KNOWLEDGE

A PRACTICAL GUIDE TO INNER PEACE

A Toltec
Wisdom Book

THE VOICE OF
KNOWLEDGE

DON MIGUEL RUIZ

WITH JANET MILLS

AMBER-ALLEN PUBLISHING
SAN RAFAEL, CALIFORNIA

Published by Amber-Allen Publishing, Inc.
Post Office Box 6657
San Rafael, California 94903

Editorial: Janet Mills
Typography: Rick Gordon, Emerald Valley Graphics
Cover Art: Nicholas Wilton, Studio Zocolo
Author Photo: Ellen Denuto

Library of Congress Cataloging-in-Publication Data
Ruiz, Miguel, 1952- The voice of knowledge : a practical guide
to inner peace / Miguel Ruiz with Janet Mills.
p. cm. -- (A Toltec wisdom book)
ISBN 978-1-878424-54-9 (pbk. : alk. paper)
I. Conduct of life. 2. Peace of mind. 3. Toltec philosophy.
I. Mills, Janet, 1953- II. Title II. Series: Ruiz, Miguel, 1952- .
Toltec wisdom book.
BJ1595.R745 2004
299.7'92--dc22   2004045051

Printed in Canada
Distributed by Publishers Group West

20 19 18 17 16 15 14 13 12 11 10 9 8 7 6

I dedicate this book to the angels who have
helped to spread the message of truth
all around the world.

CONTENTS

Contents

Acknowledgments

I WISH TO EXPRESS MY GRATITUDE TO JANET MILLS, the mother of this book. I would also like to thank Gabrielle Rivera, Gail Mills, and Nancy Carleton, who lovingly and generously contributed their time and talents to the realization of this book.

The Toltec

THOUSANDS OF YEARS AGO, THE TOLTEC WERE KNOWN throughout southern Mexico as "women and men of knowledge." Anthropologists have spoken of the Toltec as a nation or a race, but, in fact, the Toltec were scientists and artists who formed a society to explore and conserve the spiritual knowledge and practices of the ancient ones. They came together as masters (*naguals*) and students at Teotihuacan, the ancient city of pyramids outside Mexico City known as the place where "Man Becomes God."

Over the millennia, the *naguals* were forced to conceal the ancestral wisdom and maintain its existence in obscurity. European conquest, coupled with rampant misuse of personal power by a few of the apprentices, made it necessary to shield the knowledge from those who were not prepared to use it wisely or who might intentionally misuse it for personal gain.

Fortunately, the esoteric Toltec knowledge was embodied and passed on through generations by different lineages of *naguals.* Though it remained veiled in secrecy for hundreds of years, ancient prophecies foretold the coming of an age when it would be necessary to return the wisdom to the people. Now, don Miguel Ruiz, a *nagual* from the Eagle Knight lineage, has been guided to share with us the powerful teachings of the Toltec.

Toltec knowledge arises from the same essential unity of truth as all the sacred esoteric traditions found around the world. Though it is not a religion, it honors all the spiritual masters who have taught on the earth. While it does embrace spirit, it is most accurately described as a way of life, distinguished by the ready accessibility of happiness and love.

THE VOICE OF
KNOWLEDGE

What is truth is real.

What is not truth is not real.

It's an illusion, but it looks real.

Love is real.

It's the supreme expression of life.

1

ADAM AND EVE

The story from a different point of view

A BEAUTIFUL AND ANCIENT LEGEND THAT ALMOST everyone has heard before is the story of Adam and Eve. It is one of my favorite stories because it explains with symbolism what I will try to explain with words. The story of Adam and Eve is based on absolute truth, though I never understood it as a child. It is one of the greatest teachings ever, but

I believe that most people misunderstand it. Now I will tell you this story from a different point of view, perhaps from the same point of view as the one who created it.

The story is about you and me. It's about us. It's about all of humanity because, as you know, humanity is only one living being: man, woman — we are only one. In this story, we call ourselves Adam and Eve, and we are the original humans.

The story begins when we were innocent, before we closed our spiritual eyes, which means thousands of years ago. We used to live in Paradise, in the Garden of Eden, which was heaven on earth. Heaven exists when our spiritual eyes are open. It is a place of peace and joy, freedom and eternal love.

For us — Adam and Eve — everything was about love. We loved and respected one another, and we lived in perfect harmony with all of creation. Our relationship with God, our Creator, was a perfect communion of love, which means that we communed with God all of the time, and God communed with us. It was inconceivable to be afraid of God, the one who created us. Our Creator was a God of love and justice, and we put our faith and trust in God. God gave us complete freedom, and we used our free will to love and enjoy all of creation. Life was beautiful in Paradise. The original humans saw everything through the eyes of truth, the way *it is*, and we loved it. That is the way we used to be, and it was effortless.

Well, the legend says that in the middle of Paradise stood two trees. One was the Tree of Life, which gave life to everything in existence, and the other was the Tree of Death, better known as the Tree of Knowledge. The Tree of Knowledge was a beautiful tree with juicy fruit. Very tempting. And God told us, "Don't go near the Tree of Knowledge. If you eat the fruit of that tree, you may die."

Of course, no problem. But by nature we love to explore, and surely we went to pay a visit to the tree. If you remember the story, you can already guess who lived in that tree. The Tree of Knowledge was the home of a big snake full of poison. The snake is just another symbol for what the Toltec call the *Parasite*, and you can imagine why.

The story says that the snake who lived in the Tree of Knowledge was a fallen angel who used to be the most beautiful one. As you know, an angel is a messenger who delivers God's message — a message of truth and love. But for who knows what reason, that fallen angel no longer delivered the truth, which means he delivered the wrong message. The fallen angel's message was fear, instead of love; it was a lie, instead of truth. In fact, the story describes the fallen angel as the Prince of Lies, which means that he was an eternal liar. Every word coming out of his mouth was a lie.

According to the story, the Prince of Lies was living in the Tree of Knowledge, and the fruit of that tree, which was *knowledge*, was contaminated with lies. We went to that tree, and we had the most incredible conversation with the Prince of Lies. We were innocent. We didn't know. We trusted everyone. And there was the Prince of Lies, the first storyteller, a very smart guy. Now the story gets a little more interesting because that snake by itself had a whole story of its own.

That fallen angel talked and talked and talked, and we listened and listened and listened. As you know, when we are children and our grandparents tell us stories, we are eager to hear everything they tell us. We learn, and it's very seductive; we want to know more. But this was the Prince of Lies talking. No doubt about it — he was lying, and we were seduced by the lies. We *believed* the fallen angel's story, and that was our big mistake. That is what it means to eat the fruit of the Tree of Knowledge. We *agreed* and took his word as the truth. We *believed* the lies; we put our *faith* in them.

When we bit into the apple, we ate the lies that came with knowledge. What happens when we eat a lie? We believe it, and boom! Now that lie lives in us. This is easy to understand. The mind is very fertile ground for concepts, ideas, and opinions. If someone tells us a lie and we believe it, that lie takes root in our mind. There it can grow big and strong, just like a tree. One little lie can be very contagious, spreading its seeds from person to person when we share it with others. Well, the lies went into our mind, and reproduced a whole Tree of Knowledge inside our head, which is everything that we know. But what is it that we know? Mostly lies.

The Tree of Knowledge is a powerful symbol. The legend says that whoever eats the fruit of the Tree of Knowledge will have knowledge of good and evil; they will know the difference between what is right and what is wrong, what is beautiful and what is ugly. They will gather all of that knowledge and begin to judge. Well, that is what happened in our head. And the symbolism of the apple is that every concept, every lie, is just like a fruit with a seed. When we place a fruit in fertile ground, the seed of the fruit creates another tree. That tree reproduces more fruit, and by the fruit, we know the tree.

Now each of us has our own Tree of Knowledge, which is our personal belief system. The Tree of

Knowledge is the structure of everything we believe. Every concept, every opinion, forms a little branch of that tree, until we end up with the whole Tree of Knowledge. As soon as that Tree is alive in our mind, we hear the fallen angel talking very loudly. The same fallen angel, the Prince of Lies, lives in our mind. From the Toltec point of view, a Parasite was living in the fruit; we ate the fruit, and the Parasite went inside us. Now the Parasite is living our life. The storyteller, the Parasite, is born inside our head, and it survives inside our head because we feed it with our faith.

The story of Adam and Eve explains how humanity fell from the dream of heaven into the dream of hell; it tells us how we became the way we are right now. The story usually says that we took just one bite of the apple, but this is not true. I think we ate all of the fruit of that tree, and we became sick from being so full of lies and emotional poison. Humans ate every concept, every opinion, and every story the liar told us, even though it was not the truth.

In that moment, our spiritual eyes closed, and we could no longer see the world with the eyes of truth. We began to perceive the world in a completely different way, and everything changed for us. With the Tree of Knowledge in our head, we could only perceive knowledge, we could only perceive lies. We no longer lived in heaven because lies have no place in heaven. This is how humans lost Paradise: We dream lies. We create the whole dream of humanity, individually and collectively, based on lies.

Before humans ate the fruit of the Tree of Knowledge, we lived in truth. We spoke only truth. We lived in love without any fear. After we ate the fruit, we felt guilt and shame. We judged ourselves as no longer good enough, and of course we judged others the same way. With judgment came polarity, separation, and the need to punish and be punished. For the first time we were no longer kind to one another; we no longer respected and loved all of God's creation. Now we suffered, and we began to blame ourselves, to blame other people, and even to blame God. We no longer believed that God was loving and just; we believed that God would punish and hurt us. It was a lie. It was not true, but we believed it, and we separated from God.

From this point, it is easy to understand what is meant by *original sin*. The original sin is not sex. No, that is another lie. The original sin is to believe the lies that come from the snake in the tree, the fallen angel. The meaning of the word *sin* is "to go against." Everything that we say, everything that we do against ourselves is a sin. To sin is not about blame or moral condemnation. To sin is to believe in lies, and to use those lies against ourselves. From that first sin, that original lie, all of our other sins are born.

How many lies do you hear in your head? Who is judging, who is talking, who is the one with all the opinions? If you don't love, it's because that voice doesn't let you love. If you don't enjoy your life, it's because that voice doesn't let you enjoy it.

And not only that — the liar in our head has the need to express all those lies, to tell its story. We share the fruit of our Tree with others, and because others have the same kind of liar, together our lies become more powerful. Now we can hate more. Now we can hurt more. Now we can defend our lies and become fanatics following our lies. Humans even destroy one another in the name of these lies. Who is living our life? Who is making our choices? I think the answer is obvious.

Now we know what is going on in our head. The storyteller is there; it is that voice in our head. That voice is talking and talking and talking, and we are listening and listening and believing every word. That voice never stops judging. It judges whatever we do, whatever we don't do, whatever we feel, whatever we don't feel, whatever everybody else does. It is constantly gossiping in our head, and what comes out of that voice? Lies, mostly lies.

These lies hook our attention, and all we can see are lies. That is the reason we don't see the reality of heaven that exists in this same place, at this same time. Heaven belongs to us because we are the children of heaven. The voice in our head doesn't belong to us. When we are born, we don't have that voice. The voice in our head comes after we learn — first the language, then different points of view, then all the judgments and lies. Even when we first learn to speak, we speak only truth. But little by little, the whole Tree of Knowledge is programmed into our head, and the big liar eventually takes over the dream of our life.

You see, in the moment when we separated from God, we started to search for God. For the first time, we started to search for the love we believed we didn't have. We started to search for justice, for beauty, for truth. The search began thousands of years ago, and humans are still searching for the paradise we lost. We are searching for the way we used to be before we believed in lies: authentic, truthful, loving, joyful. The truth is we are searching for our Self.

You know, it was true what God told us: If we eat the fruit of the Tree of Knowledge, we may die. We did eat it, and we are dead. We are dead because our authentic self is no longer there. The one who is living our life is the big liar, the Prince of Lies, that voice in our head. You can call it *thinking*. I call it *the voice of knowledge*.

❧

Points to Ponder

• The mind is fertile ground for concepts, ideas, and opinions. If someone tells us a lie and we believe it, that lie takes root in our mind and can grow big and strong, like a tree. One little lie can be very contagious, spreading its seeds from person to person when we share it with others.

• Knowledge goes into our mind and reproduces a structure inside our head, which is everything that we know. With all that knowledge in our head, we only perceive what we *believe*; we only perceive our own knowledge. And what is it that we know? Mostly lies.

• Once the Tree of Knowledge is alive in our mind, we hear the fallen angel talking very loudly. That voice never stops judging. It tells us what is right and what is wrong, what is beautiful and what is ugly. The storyteller is born inside our head, and survives inside our head because we feed it with our faith.

• Heaven exists when our spiritual eyes are open, when we perceive the world through the eyes of truth. Once lies hook our attention, our spiritual eyes are closed. We fall from the dream of heaven and begin to live the dream of hell.

• Heaven belongs to us because we are the children of heaven. The voice in our head doesn't belong to us. When we are born, we don't have that voice. *Thinking* comes after we learn — first the language, then different points of view, then all the judgments and lies. *The voice of knowledge* comes as we accumulate knowledge.

• Before we eat the lies that come with knowledge, we live in truth. We speak only truth. We live in love without any fear. Once we have knowledge, we judge ourselves as no longer good enough; we feel guilt, shame, and the need to be punished. We begin to dream lies, and we separate from God.

• In the moment when we separate from God, we begin to search for God, for the love we believe we don't have. Humans are continually searching for justice, for beauty, for truth — for the way we used to be before we believed in lies. We are searching for our authentic self.

2

A VISIT WITH GRANDFATHER

A simple truth is discovered

I CONSIDER MYSELF LUCKY BECAUSE I GREW UP learning from an ancient tradition known as the Toltec. My mother was a great healer, and to witness miracles was nothing extraordinary because I didn't know anything else. I grew up believing that anything is possible, but what I learned about the Toltec was full of superstition and mythology. I remember seeing superstitions everywhere, and as a teenager, I began to rebel against all of the lies that come from this tradition. I learned to challenge everything until certain experiences opened my eyes to the truth. Then I knew that what I had learned from the ancient Toltec was no longer a theory. I knew, but I could not explain it with words.

In this book, I want to tell you about some of the experiences that changed my point of view completely. With each experience, I realized something that was always obvious, but that I had never seen before. Perhaps the way I will relate these stories to you is not exactly the way they happened, but it's the way I perceive them and try to explain them to myself. Maybe you have had similar moments when you realized, as I did, that most of what we believe is not the truth. Opportunities to perceive the truth always come to us, and my life has been full of these opportunities. Many of them I just let go, but others opened my spiritual eyes and made the transformation in my life possible.

One of these opportunities came from a visit with my grandfather when I was a teenager in college. My grandfather was what they call an old *nagual*, which is like a shaman. He was close to ninety years old, and people used to visit with him just to learn, just to be around him. Grandfather had been teaching me since I was a child, and I had worked hard all my youth to be good enough to earn his respect.

Well, this was a time when I was pretending to be an intellectual, and I wanted to impress my grandfather with my opinions about everything I was learning in school. I was ready to show the one who had been the biggest influence on my life how smart I was. Good luck! I went to my grandfather's house, and he received me the way he always did — with a big smile, with enormous love. I started to tell him my point of view about all of the injustice in the world, about the poverty, about the violence, about the conflict between good and what I then called *evil*.

My grandfather was very patient, and he listened very carefully to everything I said. This encouraged me to speak even more, just to impress him. At a certain point, I saw a little smile on his face. Ooh! I knew something was coming. I was not impressing him at all. I thought, "Oh, he's making fun of me." He noticed my reaction, and looked directly into my eyes. "Well, Miguel, those are very good theories that you've learned," he said. "But they are only theories. Everything you have told me is just a story. It doesn't mean that it's true."

Of course I felt a little badly about this. I took it personally right away, and I tried to defend my point of view. But it was too late because now my grandfather started to talk. He looked at me with a big smile and said, "You know, most people around the world believe that there is a great conflict in the universe, a conflict between good and evil. Well, this is not true. It's true that there is a conflict, but the conflict only exists in the human mind, not in the universe. It's not true for the plants or the animals. It's not true for the stars or the trees, or for the rest of nature. It's only true for humans. And the conflict in the human mind is not really between good and evil. The real conflict in our mind is between the truth and what is not the truth, between the truth and lies. Good and evil are just the result of that conflict. The result of believing in the truth is goodness, love, happiness. When you live your life in truth, you feel good, and your life is wonderful. The result of believing in lies and defending those lies creates what you call *evil*; it creates fanaticism. Believing in lies creates all of the injustice, all of the violence and abuse, all of the suffering, not only in society but also in the individual. The universe is as simple as *it is* or *it is not*, but humans complicate everything."

Hmm. . . . What my grandfather told me was logical, and I understood what he was saying, but I didn't believe him. How could all of the conflict in the world, all of the war, violence, and injustice, be the result of something so simple? Surely it must be more complicated than that.

Grandfather went on to say, "Miguel, all of the drama you suffer in your personal life is the result of believing in lies, mainly about yourself. And the first lie you believe is you *are not:* You *are not* the way you should be, you *are not* good enough, you *are not* perfect. We are born perfect, we grow up perfect, and we will die perfect, because only perfection exists. But the big lie is that you are not perfect, that nobody is perfect. So you start to search for an *image* of perfection that you can never become. You will never reach perfection in that way because that image is false. It's a lie, but you invest your faith in that lie, and then you build a whole structure of lies to support it."

In that moment I didn't realize that my grandfather had given me a great opportunity — something as simple as having the awareness that every drama in my life, all of the suffering in my life, was because I believed in lies. Though I wanted to believe what my grandfather said, I only pretended to believe him. And it was so logical that I said, "Oh yes, Grandfather, you're right. I agree with you." But I was lying. There were too many lies inside my head to accept something as simple as the truth.

Then my grandfather looked at me very kindly and said, "Miguel, I can see that you are trying hard to impress me, to prove that you are good enough for me. And you have the need to do this because you are not good enough for yourself." Ouch. He got me right there. I didn't know why, but I felt as if he had caught me in a lie. I never realized that my grandfather knew about my insecurities, about the self-judgment and self-rejection, about the guilt and shame I felt. How did he know that I was pretending to be what I was not?

Grandfather was smiling again as he told me, "Miguel, everything you've learned in school, everything you know about life, is only knowledge. How can you know if what you've learned is the truth or not? How can you know if what you believe about yourself is the truth?" At that point I reacted and said, "Of course I know the truth about myself. I live with myself every day. I know what I am!" Grandfather really laughed at that and said, "The truth is that you have no idea what you really are, but you know what you *are not*. You have been practicing what you *are not* for so long, that you really believe your *image* is what you are. Your faith is invested in all those lies you believe about yourself. It's a story, but it's not the truth.

"Miguel, what makes you powerful is your faith. Faith is the power of creation that all humans have, and it doesn't have anything to do with religion. Faith is the result of an agreement. When you agree to believe in something without a doubt, you invest your faith. If you have no doubt about what you believe, then for you it is truth, even though it may really be a lie. Your faith is so powerful that if you believe you are not good enough, you are not good enough! If you believe you will fail, you will fail, because that is the power and magic of your faith. As I said before, you suffer because you believe lies. It's that simple. Humanity is the way it is because collectively we believe so many lies. Humans have carried the lies for thousands of years, and we react to the lies with hate, with anger, with violence. But they're only lies."

I was wondering, "Then how can we know the truth?" Before I could ask this question out loud, my grandfather answered it: "The truth needs to be experienced. Humans have the need to describe, to explain, to express what we perceive, but when we experience the truth, there are no words to describe it. Whoever claims, 'This is the truth,' is lying without even knowing it. We can perceive truth with our feelings, but as soon as we try to describe it with words, we distort it, and it's no longer the truth. It's our story! It's a projection based on reality that is only true for us, but still we try to put our experience into words, and this is something wonderful, really. It's the greatest art of every human."

Grandfather could see that what he had just said wasn't clear to me. "Miguel, if you are an artist, a painter, you try to express what you perceive through your art. What you paint may not be exactly what you perceive, but it is close enough to remind you of what you perceive. Well, imagine that you are very lucky and you are Pablo Picasso's friend. And because

Picasso loves you, he decides to make a portrait of you. You pose for Picasso, and after many days, he finally shows you your portrait. You will say, 'This is not me,' and Picasso will say, 'Of course it is you. This is how I see you.' For Picasso, this is true; he is expressing what he is perceiving. But you will say, 'I don't look like that.'

"Well, every human is the same as Picasso. Every human is a storyteller, which means that every human is an artist. What Picasso does with colors, we do with words. Humans witness life happening inside us and all around us, and we use words to make a portrait of what we witness. Humans make up stories about everything we perceive, and just like Picasso we distort the truth; but for us, it *is* the truth. Of course, the way we express our distortion could be something other people enjoy. Picasso's art is highly valued by many people.

"All humans create their story with their own unique point of view. Why try to impose your story on other people when for them your story is not true? When you understand that, you no longer have the need to defend what you believe. It's not important to be right or to make others wrong. Instead, you see everybody as an artist, a storyteller. You know that whatever they believe is just their point of view. It has nothing to do with you."

Well, I had wanted to impress my grandfather, but he had impressed me once again. I had so much respect for my elders. Later in my life I understood the smile on my grandfather's face. He had not been making fun of me. The smile was because I reminded him of a time when, just like me, he had tried to impress his elders.

After this conversation with my grandfather, I felt the need to make sense of things. I wanted to understand my personal life, and to find out when I began to invest my faith in lies. It was not easy. That conversation took me years to digest. To see myself in the present moment, to see what I believed, was not that obvious and not so easy to give up. But I wanted answers because this is my nature. I needed to know, and the only point of reference was my memories.

❧

POINTS TO PONDER

• There is a conflict in the human mind between the truth and what is not the truth, between the truth and lies. The result of believing in the truth is goodness, love, happiness. The result of believing and defending lies is injustice and suffering — not only in society, but also in the individual.

• All of the drama humans suffer is the result of believing in lies, mainly about ourselves. The first lie we believe is *I am not:* I am not the way I *should* be, I am not perfect. The truth is that every human is born perfect because only perfection exists.

• We humans have no idea what we really are, but we know what we *are not*. We create an image of perfection, a story about what we *should* be, and we begin to search for a false image. The image is a lie, but we invest our faith in that lie. Then we build a whole structure of lies to support it.

• Faith is a powerful force in humans. If we invest our faith in a lie, that lie becomes truth for us. If we believe we are not good enough, then *thy will be done*, we are not good enough. If we believe we will fail, we will fail, because that is the power and magic of our faith.

• Humans can perceive truth with our feelings, but when we try to describe the truth, we can only tell a story that we distort with our word. The story may be true for us, but that doesn't mean it is true for anyone else.

• All humans are storytellers with their own unique point of view. When we understand this, we no longer feel the need to impose our story on others or to defend what we believe. Instead, we see all of us as artists with the right to create our own art.

3

THE LIE OF OUR IMPERFECTION

Childhood memories are recalled

I REMEMBER WHEN I WAS A CHILD. I WAS SO FREE. It was wonderful to be a child. I remember that I learned to walk before I learned to talk. I was like a little sponge trying to learn everything. I also remember the way I used to be before I learned to speak.

As a little child I was completely authentic. I never pretended to be what I am not. My tendency was to play, to explore, to be happy. My emotions ruled everything. I only wanted to do what I liked to do, and I tried to avoid what I didn't like. All of my attention was focused on what I was feeling, and I could perceive the emotions coming out of other people. We can call it *instinct* if we want to, but it was a kind of perception. Some people I would run to because I trusted them. I wouldn't get close to others because I felt uncomfortable. I had many emotions that I couldn't explain because I didn't have words, of course.

I remember waking up, seeing my mother's face, and feeling overwhelmed with a desire to grab her. I didn't know that this emotion was called *love*. It was completely natural to love. I felt the same way about my toys, and about the cat and the dog, too. I remember seeing my father come back from work and running to him and jumping on him with so much joy, with a big and beautiful smile. Completely authentic. I could be naked and I didn't care what people thought. I used to be myself, whatever

I was, because I didn't have *knowledge*. I didn't have a program in my head. I didn't know what I was, and I didn't care to know. Just as a dog doesn't know that it's a dog. But it acts like a dog. Barks like a dog. Well, I used to be like that. I lived my life through my integrity. This was my true nature before I learned to speak.

I continued to explore my childhood memories, and I discovered that something happens to all of us. What happens? Well, knowledge happens. I can remember starting to learn words. I learn the names of every object I perceive. I learn a language, which is great. Now I can use words to ask for what I want. Months later, or maybe years later, my mind is mature enough for abstract concepts. With these concepts, something incredible happens. I start to create stories by qualifying everything: what is right or wrong, what I should or shouldn't be, what is good or bad, beautiful or ugly. I learn from my parents not just what they say, but what they do. I learn what they say not just to me, but what they say about other people. I learn how to interact. I copy everything that I see. I see my father, very powerful, with his strong opinions, and I want to be like him. I can hardly wait to grow up to have an opinion of my own.

When I finally understand the language, almost everybody begins to tell me what I am. The way I learn about myself is by hearing the opinions of the storytellers around me. My mother creates an image of me based on what she believes I am. She tells me what I am, and I believe her. Then my father tells me what I am, and it's something completely different, but I agree with him, too. Of course, each of my brothers and sisters has an opinion of me, and I agree with them. Surely they know more than I do, even though I'm the one who lives in this physical body. None of this makes sense, but I'm having fun.

Then I go to school, and the teacher tells me what I am, which is still okay until she tells me the way I should be, but *I am not.* I agree, and the problem begins in that moment. I hear the teacher say,

"Children, you need to work hard to become somebody, to be a success in life. The world is divided into winners and losers, and you are here to prepare yourself to become a winner. If you work hard, perhaps you will be a lawyer, a doctor, an engineer." My teacher tells me stories about all of the past presidents and what they did when they were children. Of course all of the heroes are winners. I am a child; I am innocent. I learn the concept of *winner*. I agree that I should become a winner, and that's it — that agreement is stored in my memory.

At home, I hear my parents say, "Miguel, you have to behave this way to be a good boy," which means that if I don't behave that way, *I am not* a good boy. They don't say this, but I understand this. You have to do this, this, and that to be a good boy. Then you will get a reward. And if you are not that way, you will be punished. Oops! I am too small; they are so big. I try to rebel, and I fail. They win. I start pretending to be what *I am not* to avoid the punishment, but also to get the reward. I have to be what they tell me to be because the reward only goes to good boys. I remember trying so hard to become what they want me to be, just to have the reward of their attention, just to hear them say, "Miguel, you are such a good boy."

What I don't notice behind all of the messages I hear are the silent messages that are never said, but that I can understand: *I am not the way I should be; it is not okay to be me.* If the message is "Miguel, you have to work hard to become somebody," that means that right now I am nobody. In a child's mind the silent message I understand is *I am not good enough.* And not just that; I never will be good enough because *I am not perfect.* I agree, and in that moment, like most of us, I start searching for perfection.

That's how the image of perfection is introduced in my mind. This is when I stop being myself, and start pretending to be what *I am not.* That first lie happens in my first year of school, almost right away. Sitting in that classroom and seeing my first teacher impresses me deeply. The teacher is a grown-up.

Whatever she says must be the truth, just as whatever my father or mother says must be the truth. She is a great teacher who really cares about children, and even though the message I receive is mostly positive, the consequence is a little different. Behind that message is something very subtle. I call it *the lie of my imperfection.* It is the main lie that I agree to believe about myself, and from that lie, more lies are invented to support it.

This is the moment of my fall, when I start to come out of heaven, when my faith in the lie begins to work its magic. Just like a miracle, it starts to take effect all around me: I have to work hard to be good enough for my mother, to be good enough for my father, to be good enough for my older brothers and sisters, to be good enough for my teachers. This is overwhelming, but it's not over yet. I turn on the television and they also tell me the way I should look, the way I should dress, the way I should be, but *I am not.* Television gives me more images of heroes and villains. I see people trying hard to be winners. I see them striving for perfection, wanting to be somebody important, wanting to be what they are not.

The real drama begins when I am a teenager because now it's not only that I'm not good enough for other people; I am no longer good enough for myself. The result is self-rejection. I try to prove my worth to myself by working hard to get A's in school. I try hard to be the best at sports, the best at playing chess, the best at everything. At first I do this to try to impress my father and my older brothers; later, I do this to impress myself. At this point, I am no longer authentic. I have lost my integrity, my authenticity, because I no longer make decisions based on what is good for me. It is more important to satisfy other people's points of view.

When I change schools from elementary to the next level, I am told, "You are not a child anymore; you cannot act like a child. Now you have to behave this way." Over and over, I try to please other people by pretending to be what they want me to be.

I start searching for opinions from everybody. How do I look? What do you think of me? Did I do a good job? I am looking for support, for someone to tell me, "Miguel, you are so good." And if I'm with somebody who tells me how good I am, that person can manipulate my life so easily because I need that recognition. I need somebody to tell me that I'm intelligent, that I'm wonderful, that I'm a winner.

I can't stand to be alone with myself. When I'm alone, I see myself as a loser, and my self-judgment is strong. Because *I am not* the way I should be according to my story, I judge myself and find myself guilty. Then I begin to use everything around me as an instrument for self-punishment. I have the tendency to compare myself with other people. "Oh, they are better than I am. Well, they are worse." That makes me feel a little better, but then I see myself in the mirror — ugh! I don't like what I see. I reject myself; of course I don't love myself. But I pretend that I love myself. With enough practice, I even begin to believe what I pretend.

Later, when I really try to prove myself in society, I become a medical doctor. Does becoming a medical doctor finally make me a winner? No, oh no. There are cardiologists, neurologists, surgeons. Then I become a surgeon, but I'm still not good enough according to my story. I have an image of myself that I believe when I'm alone, and I project different images around other people, depending on what I want them to believe about me. In trying to project my images, I have to defend these images. I have to become very intelligent just to cover all of the lies!

I keep pretending to be all of those images, and from years and years of practice, I become a great actor. If I have a broken heart, I tell myself, "It doesn't hurt. I don't care." I am lying. I am pretending. I could almost win an Academy Award for my performance. What a character, what a drama! And I could say that the drama of my life begins when I agree that I am not good enough — when I hear my teachers, my family, the television tell me, "Miguel, you have to be *this* way," but *I am not.*

I am searching for appreciation, for acceptance, for love — not knowing that it's just a story. I am searching for perfection, and I find it very interesting how "not being perfect" becomes the biggest excuse people use to justify their actions. Every time they make a mistake and need to defend their image, I hear them say, "Well, I'm only human; I'm not perfect. Only God is perfect." This also becomes the biggest excuse for every mistake I make. "Oh well, nobody's perfect." What a great justification.

I go to church, and they show me pictures of saints: "This is perfection." But in the faces of the saints I see suffering and pain. Ooh! To be perfect, do I need to be like them? Yes, I am here to suffer, and if I suffer with patience, maybe when I die I can receive my reward in heaven. Maybe then I'll be perfect!

I used to believe that because I heard it so often. But it's just a story. I had so many superstitions in my head about myself, about everything. Lies that come from thousands of years ago still affect the way we create our own story. What I was told as a child is "Only God is perfect. All of God's creation is perfect except humans." At the same time, I was told that God put humans at the very top of creation. But how can humans be at the top of creation, when everything is perfect except humans? It didn't make sense to me. After I grew up, I thought about the contradiction. This is not possible. If God is perfect, well, God is the one who creates everything. If I really believe in the perfection of God's creation, then I think that all of us are perfect or God is not perfect either.

I love and respect all of God's creation. How can I say, "God, you have created billions of people, and they are not perfect"? For me to say that I am not perfect or that you are not perfect is the greatest insult to God, from my point of view. If we don't see the perfection, it's because our attention is focused on the lie, on that image of perfection that we can never be. And how many of us give up trying to be the image of perfection, but in giving up we don't go as warriors? We just accept that we are failures, that we will never make it, and we blame everything out-side of us. "I didn't make it because nobody helped me — because of this or that or whatever." There are hundreds of excuses, but now the self-judgment is even worse than before. When we are still trying to be perfect, the judgment is there, but it's not as bad as when we give up. Then we try to cover our frus-tration, and say, "I'm okay; this is the kind of life I want," but we know that we have failed, and we can't hide what we believe from ourselves.

Of course, any time we try to be what we are not, we fail. It's so difficult to be what we are not, to *pretend* to be what we are not. I used to pretend that I was very happy and very strong and very impor-tant. Wow! Living that way is truly a deep hell. It's a setup, it's a no-win situation. You can never be what you are not, and that is the main point. You can only be *you*, and that's it. And you are *you* right now, and it's effortless.

There is no need to justify what we are. There is no need to work hard to become what we are not.

We just need to return to our integrity, to the way we were before we learned to speak. Perfect. As little children, we are authentic. When we are hungry, we only want to eat. When we are tired, we just want to rest. Only the present time is real for us; we don't care about the past, and we aren't worried about the future. We enjoy life; we want to explore and have fun. Nobody teaches us to be that way; we are born that way.

We are born in truth, but we grow up believing in lies. This is the whole drama of humanity, the whole problem with storytellers. One of the biggest lies in the story of humanity is the lie of our imperfection. That lie had a big effect in my own life. And though I tell others not to make assumptions, I have to assume that in one way or another this happens to all of us. Of course there are differences in the story, but I think the pattern is more or less the same for everyone. Hardly anyone can escape from the setup.

I was a perfect little child. I was innocent, and I ate the lie that *I am not* what I should be. I believed that I would have to work hard to become what I should be. This is how I learned to create my story, and because I had faith in the story, the story became truth for me. And the story, even if it is full of lies, is perfect. It is wonderful and beautiful. The story is not right or wrong or good or bad — it's just a story, that's all. But with awareness, we can change the story. Step by step, we can return to the truth.

POINTS TO PONDER

• As little children, we are completely authentic. We never pretend to be what we are not. Our tendency is to play and explore, to live in the moment, to enjoy life. Nobody teaches us to be that way; we are born that way. This is our true nature before we learn to speak.

• When the human mind is mature enough for abstract concepts, we learn to qualify everything: right or wrong, good or bad, beautiful or ugly. We create a story about what we *should* be, we put our faith in the story, and the story becomes the truth for us.

• Behind all of the messages that we hear as children are the silent messages that are never said, but that we can understand: *It is not okay to be me. I am not good enough.* The moment we agree, we stop being ourselves and start pretending to be what we are not, just to please other people, just to fit an image they create for us according to their story.

• You can never be what you are not. You can only be *you*, and that's it. And you are *you* right now, and it's effortless.

• Humans are born in truth, but we grow up believing in lies. One of the biggest lies in the story of humanity is the lie of our imperfection. It's just a story, but we believe it, and we use the story to judge ourselves, to punish ourselves, and to justify our mistakes.

• Everything in God's creation is perfect. If we don't see our own perfection, it's because our attention is focused on our story. The lies in our story keep us from seeing the truth. But with awareness, we can change the story and return to the truth.

4

A Night in the Desert

An encounter with the infinite

ANOTHER OPPORTUNITY TO PERCEIVE THE TRUTH came along when I was doing my social service as a medical doctor. I was in the little town of Altar Sonora in the Sonoran desert. It was summer, and the heat was so intense that I couldn't sleep. I decided to leave the clinic and take a walk in the desert. There was a new moon that night, and I could see millions of stars in the sky. I was alone in the middle of the desert, perceiving so much beauty. I saw eternity, the endless, the infinite in those stars, and I knew without a doubt that the stars are alive. The infinite, our Mother Earth, all of creation, is alive. It is one living being.

Surely I had seen those stars many times before, but never in that way, from that point of view. My emotional reaction was overwhelming. I felt intense joy mixed with the most exquisite peace in my heart. Then something incredible happened. I had the sensation that I was not alone in the desert. While I was perceiving the immensity of the infinite, the infinite was perceiving me. All of those millions of stars were part of one living being who knows everything and perceives everything. The universe knew that I existed!

Then something even more extraordinary happened. My perception shifted, and for a moment I was the immensity of the stars perceiving the infinite in my physical body. I could see myself in the middle of the desert — so small. I saw that my physical body was made of billions of tiny stars, which I knew were atoms, and they were as vast as all of the stars in the sky.

That night, I knew that the infinite inside my physical body is just a continuation of the infinite all around me. I am part of that infinite, and so is every object I perceive. There is no difference between any of us, or between us and any object. We are only one because everything is made of light. Light expresses itself in billions of different forms to create the material universe. More than that, I knew that there is only one force that moves and transforms everything. The force that moves the stars is the same force that moves the atoms in my body. I call it *life*, and light is the messenger or carrier of *life* because light is sending information all the time to everything in existence.

And it was incredible to understand that light is alive. Light is a living being that contains all of the wisdom of the universe and occupies every space. There is no empty space between the stars, just as there is no empty space between the atoms in my body. The space between the stars is filled with light; it only appears empty when there is no object to reflect the light. Any object we send into space will reflect light because all matter reflects light, just like a mirror.

Then I looked in my pocket for a little mirror that I always carried with me in my practice. In the mirror, I could see an exact copy of all of creation, a virtual reality made by light. In that moment I knew that my eyes were just like a couple of mirrors. Light projects a virtual reality inside my brain, just the way it projects a virtual reality inside a mirror. It was obvious that everything I perceive is a virtual reality made by images of light. The only difference between my eyes and a mirror is that my eyes have a brain behind them. And with that brain I have the capacity to analyze, interpret, and describe the virtual reality I perceive at any moment.

I co-create with God, with *life*. God creates what is real, and I create the virtual reality inside my mind.

Through light, life sends all of that information into my eyes, and I make a story about what I perceive. The story is how I qualify, justify, and explain what I perceive. If I see a tree, I don't just *see* the tree; I qualify the tree, I describe the tree, I have an opinion about the tree. I like the tree or I don't like the tree. I may feel that the tree is beautiful or not, but my point of view, my opinion about the tree, is a story of my own creation. Once I interpret, qualify, or judge what I perceive, it is no longer real; it is a virtual world. This is what the Toltec call *dreaming*.

Now everything started to make sense in my mind. I finally understood what my mother and my grandfather had tried to teach me for so long about the ancient philosophy of the Toltec. The Toltec believe that humans are living in a dream. The dream is a world of illusion made by images of light, and the mind dreams when the brain is both asleep and awake.

Then I remembered that the word *Toltec* means "artist of the spirit." In the Toltec tradition, every human is an artist, and the supreme art is the expression of the beauty of our spirit. If we understand this point of view, we can see how wonderful it is to call ourselves artists instead of humans. When we think of ourselves as human, we limit the way we express ourselves in life. We hear, "I'm just a human; I'm not perfect." But if we call ourselves artists, where is that limitation? As artists, we no longer have any limitation; we are creators, just like the one who created us.

The Toltec believe that the force of life working through us is what really creates the art, and that everyone is an instrument of this force. Every manifestation of the supreme artist becomes an artist itself that manifests art through its own manifestations. The art is alive, and it has self-awareness because it comes from life. The creation is ongoing, it is endless, it is happening in every moment, everywhere.

How do we live our life? This is our art, the art of living. With our power of creation, we express the force of life in everything we say, everything we feel, everything we do. But there are two kinds of artists: the ones who create their story without awareness, and the ones who recover awareness and create their story with truth and with love.

You are dreaming your life in this moment. You perceive not only your own dream, but the dream of the supreme artist reflected in everything you perceive. You react and try to make sense of what you perceive. You try to explain it in your own way, depending on the knowledge stored in the memory of your mind. This is something wonderful from my point of view. You live in the story that you create, and I live in the story that I create. Your story is your reality — a virtual reality that is only true for you, the one who creates it.

Long ago, somebody said, "Every head is a world," and it's true. You live in your own world, and that world is so private. Nobody knows what you have in your world. Only you know, and some-times even you don't know. Your world is your creation, and it's a masterpiece of art.

That night in the Sonoran desert changed the way I perceive myself and humanity, the way I perceive the entire world. In a moment of inspiration, I saw the infinite, the force of life in action. That force is always present and obvious for anyone to see, but there was no way I could see it with my attention focused on lies. What my grandfather had tried to tell me was true: "Only perfection exists." It took a long time for me to put it into words, of course, but I finally understood what he meant when I experienced this truth for myself. I realized that I am perfect because I am inseparable from the infinite, the force of life that creates the stars and the entire universe of light. I am God's creation. I don't need to be what *I am not.*

This was my reencounter with love, which is how I felt before I denied myself love. I recovered my authenticity, which is how I lived before I learned any lies. In that moment of inspiration everything made sense to me without thinking at all. I was pure awareness. I was perceiving with my feelings, and if

I had tried to use words to explain what I felt, the experience would have been over.

I believe that all humans have moments of inspiration when we perceive truth. These moments usually occur when the mind is quiet — when we perceive the force of life through our feelings. Of course, the voices inside our head that we call *thinking* will invalidate our experience almost right away. These voices will try to justify and deny what we feel. Why? Because when we witness the truth, all of the lies that we believe cannot survive. Humans are afraid of the truth, and when we say that we are afraid, the one who is speaking is the liar. Yes, because the lies that speak through that voice cannot survive the truth, and they don't want to die.

That is why it takes such courage to face our own lies, to face what we believe. The structure of our knowledge makes us feel safe. We have the need to *know*, even if what we know is not the truth. And if what we believe about ourselves is no longer true, we don't feel safe because we don't know how to be any other way. When we discover that we are not what we believe we are, the foundation of our entire reality begins to collapse. The whole story loses its meaning, and this is very frightening.

I was not afraid in the desert that night. But when I recovered, I felt fear because nothing in my story was important any longer and I still had to function in the world. Later, I discovered that I could rewrite the story of my life. I could recover the structure of what I believed and rebuild it without all the lies. Then life went on as it did before, but the lies no longer ruled my life.

POINTS TO PONDER

• Light is a living being that contains all of the wisdom of the universe and occupies every space. Light, the supreme messenger of God, constantly sends information to everything in existence, and expresses itself in billions of different forms.

• Life, the force of transformation that creates and transforms the stars, is the same force that creates and transforms the atoms in our physical body. This force is always present and obvious for us to see, but we cannot see it when our attention is focused on lies.

• Every human is a part of the infinite, and so is every object we perceive. There is no difference between any of us, or between us and any object. We are only one because everything is made of light.

• Life creates what is real, and humans create a virtual reality — a story about what is real. We perceive images of *light*, and we interpret, qualify, and judge what we perceive. This ongoing reflection in the mirror of our mind is what the Toltec call *dreaming*.

• God, the supreme artist, uses our life for the creation of art. We are the instruments through which the force of life expresses itself.

• The art of dreaming is the art of living. Everything we say and do is an expression of the force of life. The creation is ongoing. It is endless. It is happening in every moment.

5

THE STORYTELLER

Exploring the characters in the story

THAT NIGHT IN THE DESERT IS WHAT I CALL MY *return to common sense.* I had been living in a story of my own creation my entire life without even noticing it! Once I had this awareness, I started to question everything in my story. Is it true that I am what I believe I am? Is what I believe about everybody else true? I reviewed the story of my life, and

I didn't like all of the drama that I had created. I wanted to reinvent myself.

The first step was to take away from my story what I felt was not true, and to find out what was true. I discovered that what I call the *frame* of the dream is true because our Creator creates the frame, and it's the same for everybody. Our agreements about what to call the objects in the frame are also true because this is how we describe our virtual reality. The letter *A* is an *A* because we say so and we agree. The word *dog* describes a type of animal that we agree to call a *dog*.

Knowledge used in this way is just a *tool for communication.* But almost everything that is abstract is a lie: what is right or wrong, what is good or bad, what is beautiful or ugly. I discovered that more than 90 percent of the concepts I had stored in my mind were based on lies, especially the concepts I believed about myself: I can do this; I cannot do that. I am this way; I will never be that way. The problem is not really knowledge; the problem is what *contaminates* knowledge — and that is the lie. I could see that there was a lot of nonsense in the way we learn to write our stories. How did this happen?

Before I was born in this physical body, a whole society of storytellers was already here. The story was ongoing, and from their story I learned how to create my own. The storytellers who are here before us teach us how to be human. First they tell us what we are — a boy or a girl — then they tell us who we are, and who we should or shouldn't be. They teach us how to be a woman or how to be a man. They tell us to be a *proper* woman, a *decent* woman, a *strong* man, a *brave* man. They give us a name, an identity, and they tell us the role that we are playing in their story. They prepare us to live in the human jungle, to compete with one another, to control one another, to impose our will, to fight against our own kind.

Of course I believed what the storytellers told me. Why would I not believe them? They filled me with knowledge, and I used that knowledge to copy their style and create my art in a similar way. I heard my older brothers sharing their strong opinions with my father. I tried to talk, and they shut me up right away — forget it, I had no voice. As I said before, I could hardly wait to have an opinion of my own. It didn't matter what the opinion was; I just wanted to impose my opinion and to defend my opinion with all of that self-righteousness.

As children, we witness the way other people relate to one another, and this becomes normal behavior for us. We see our older sisters and brothers, our aunts and uncles, our parents and neighbors in romantic relationships. They suffer, but they believe they love. We see them fight, and we can't wait to grow up and do the same thing. The mentality when we are children is "Wow, that looks like fun!" All of the drama we suffer in our relationships is because we witness so many lies when we are innocent, and we use these lies to form our own story.

I continued to study the story of my life, and what I discovered is that everything in my story is about me. Of course, it has to be that way because I am the center of my perception, and the story is from my point of view. The main character who lives in my story is based on someone who really exists — that is true. But what I believe about me is not true — it's a story. I create the character of "Miguel," and it's just an image based on what I agree to believe about myself. I project my image to other people in society, and other people perceive that projection, modify it, and react to me according to their stories.

Then I discovered that because it's my story, I also create an image for every secondary character who lives in my story. The secondary characters are based on people who really exist, but everything I believe about them is a story of my own creation. I create the character of my mother, the character of my father, the character of each of my brothers and sisters, my friends, my beloved, even my dog and my cat. I meet a person; I qualify the person. I make judgments about the person based on all of the knowledge in my mind. This is how I keep their image in my memory.

In my story, you are a secondary character who is my creation, and I interact with you. You project what you want me to believe about you, and I modify it depending on what I believe. Now I am sure that you are what I believe you are. I might even say, "I know you," when the truth is that I don't know you at all. I only know the story I create about you. And it took some time for me to understand that I only know the story I create about myself.

For years I thought that I knew myself until I discovered that it was not the truth. I only knew what I believed about myself. Then I discovered that I am not what I believe I am! And it was very interesting, and also very frightening, when I discovered that I really don't know anybody, and they don't know me either.

The truth is that we only know what we *know*, and the only thing we really know is our story. But how many times have you heard people say, "I know my children very well; they would never do something like that!" Do you think that you really know your children? Do you think that you really know your partner? Well, you are probably certain that your partner doesn't know you! You may be certain that nobody really knows you, but do you really know yourself? Do you really know anybody?

I used to believe that I knew my mother, but the only thing I know about her is the role I assign her to play in my story. I have an image for the character who plays the role of my mother. Everything I know about her is what I *believe* about her. I have no idea what she has in her head. Only my mother knows what she is, and surely she doesn't know either.

The same is true for you. Your mother can swear that she knows you very well. But is it true? I don't think so. You know that she has no idea what you have in your mind. She only knows what she believes about you, which means she knows almost nothing. You are a secondary character in her story, and you play the role of the son or the daughter. Your mother creates an image of you, and she wants you to fit the image she creates. If you are not what she wants you to be according to her story, guess what happens? She feels hurt by you, and she tries to make you fit her image. That is why she feels the need to control you, to tell you what to do and what not to do, to give you all of her opinions about the way you should live your life.

When you know that it's just her story, why bother defending your point of view? It doesn't matter what you say; she will not believe you anyway. How can she believe your story when it isn't her point of view? The best you can do is to change the conversation, enjoy her presence, and love her the way she is. When you have this awareness, you will forgive your mother for whatever she did to you, according to your story, of course. Just through the act of forgiveness, your relationship with your mother will change completely.

Once I discovered that people are creating and living in their own story, how could I judge them any longer? How could I take anything personally when I know that I am only a secondary character in their story? I know that when they talk to me they are really talking to the secondary character in their story. And whatever people say about me is just a projection of their *image* of me. It has nothing to do with me. I don't waste my time taking anything personally. I focus my attention on creating my own story.

Each of us has the right to create our own life story, to express ourselves through our art. But how many times do we try to make the secondary characters in our story fit the images and roles we create for them? We want our children to be the way we want them to be. Well, bad news! That will never happen. And when our partner doesn't fit the image we create for him or her, we feel angry or hurt. Then we try to control our partner; we have to tell our partner what to do, what not to do, what to believe, what not to believe. We even tell our partner how to walk, how to dress, how to speak. We do the same thing with our children, and it becomes a war of control.

Life in this physical body is very short, even if we live to be one hundred years old. When I discovered this, I decided not to waste my time creating conflict, mainly with the people I love. I want to enjoy them, and I do that by loving them for who they are, not for what they believe. The story they create is not important. I don't care if my mother's story doesn't agree with my story; I love her and I enjoy her presence. I know not to impose my story on her; I don't impose my story on anybody. I respect her story, I listen to her story, and I don't make it wrong.

If other people try to write your story, it means they don't respect you. They don't respect you because they consider that you are not a good artist, that you cannot write your own story, even though you were born to write your own story. Respect comes directly from love; it is one of the greatest expressions of love.

I also respect myself, and I don't allow anybody to write my story. My story is my responsibility; it's my creation. I am the artist, and I respect my own art. I can compare my art with other people's art, but I make my own choices, and I take responsibility for my creation. When I first had the awareness that I didn't like my story, I thought, "Okay, I am the author. I will change my story." And I tried and I failed. And I tried again and I failed again many times because I was trying to change all of the secondary characters in my story. I thought that if I changed the secondary characters, I was changing my story, and it was not true at all!

The problem is not with the secondary characters in our story. What we see in them is just a projection of what we believe, and that's a secondary problem. Our main problem is with the main character of the story. If we don't like our story, it's because we don't like what we believe about the main character. There is only one way to change our story, and that is by changing what we believe about ourselves.

This is a big step in awareness. If we clean up the lies that we believe about ourselves, almost like magic the lies that we believe about everybody else will change. Then the secondary characters in our story will change, but this doesn't mean that we exchange one person for another person. The secondary characters stay the same; what changes is what we *believe* about them. This changes what we project onto them, and with that change, the interaction we have with them changes. And with that change, the way they perceive us changes. And with that change, the secondary character who we represent in their story changes. Just like a wave that ripples across the water, we change ourselves, and everything else changes.

You are the only one who can change your story, and you do this by changing your relationship with yourself. Every time you change the main character in your story, just like magic the whole story starts to change in order to adapt to the new main character. This is easy to prove because the main character is changing anyway, but it's changing by itself, without your awareness.

The way you perceive the world when you are eight or nine years old is not the same way you perceive the world at fifteen or sixteen. When you are in your early twenties, your perception changes again. You see the world differently when you are first married, or when you have your first child. You change what you *believe* about yourself. Your point of view changes, the way you express yourself changes, and your reactions change. Everything changes, and the change can be so dramatic that it seems like two different dreams and two different people.

You also change the secondary characters in your story. The way you see your father and your mother when you are ten changes when you are twenty, and thirty, and forty, and it keeps changing. Every single day, you rewrite the story. As soon as you wake up in the morning, you have to find out what day it is. You have to find out where you are and where the story was before you went to sleep just to keep going with the story, with your life. You have to go to work, you have to do whatever activity you have planned for that day, and you keep writing your own story, but without awareness.

Everything in your story is constantly changing, including the story you tell yourself about who you are. Twenty years ago, the storyteller told you who you are, and you believed it. Today the storyteller is telling you another story about yourself, and it's completely different. Of course the storyteller will say, "Oh, that's because I have more experience. Now I know more; now I am wiser." It's just another story. Your whole life has been a story.

If you talk about something that happened to you when you were a child, your father or mother or brother or sister will have a different story. This is because we only share the frame of the dream. If two of you start talking about something that happened twenty years ago, it may sound as if you are talking about two different events. Your father claims, "This is what happened; this is the truth." And you say, "No, no, no; you're wrong. This is what really happened." Who is right and who is wrong? Well, both of you are right, according to your stories.

If one hundred people perceive the same event,

you hear one hundred different stories, and everybody claims that his or her story is the true story. Of course, it's only true for that person, and your story is only true for you. But the voice of knowledge starts searching for everything in your mind to make yourself right. You even look for allies from the outside to join you in your crusade to be right and to make the other person wrong. Why try to justify what you believe? You don't need to make others wrong because you already know that in their story they are right. In your story, you are right. Then being right or wrong is over; you no longer have to defend what you believe.

When we reach this level of awareness, it is easier not to take what other people say personally. We know that every human around us is a storyteller, and that everyone distorts the truth. What we share with one another is just our perception; it is just our point of view. And it's completely normal because the only thing we have is our point of view. This is how we describe whatever we witness.

Our point of view depends upon our programming, which is everything in our personal Tree of Knowledge. Our point of view also depends upon how we are feeling emotionally and physically, and it changes from one moment to the next. It changes when we are angry or upset, and it changes again when we are happy. Our perception changes when we are tired or hungry. We humans are constantly modifying what we say, how we react, what we project. We even modify what everybody else says!

You know, the way we create our stories is very interesting. We have a tendency to distort everything we perceive to make it agree with what we *already* believe; we "fix it" to make it agree with our lies. It is amazing how we do this. We distort the image of each of our children, we distort the image of our partner, and we distort the image of our parents. We even distort the image of our dog or our cat! People come to me and say, "Oh, I have learned so much from my dog. My dog is almost human. He's almost talking now." And they really mean it!

How many people take their dog to a pet psychologist because the dog has so many issues? Do you see how we distort our story? The story is based in reality because, yes, we have an emotional connection with our dog, but it's not true that our dog almost talks or that our dog is almost human.

When we talk about our children, we say, "My children are the best. They do this and this and that." Another person hearing this may say, "No, look at mine." As artists with our own style, we have the right to distort our story, and this is the best we can do anyway. That distortion is our point of view, and for us it has meaning. We project our story, and by seeing the distortion, we can sometimes return to our own truth. Then who says that the distortion of our story is not art? It is art, and it is beautiful.

Humans are the storytellers of God. There is something that exists inside all of us that can make an interpretation of everything we perceive. We are like God's journalists trying to explain whatever happens around us. It is our nature to make up stories, and this is why we create languages. This is why all of the world religions create beautiful mythology. We try to express what we perceive and share what we perceive, and this action is happening all of the time.

When we meet somebody new, we want to know that person's story almost right away. We ask all of the key questions: "What do you do? Where do you live? How many children do you have?" This interrogation goes both ways. We can hardly wait to tell that person our point of view, to express what we feel, to share our own story. When we experience something we like, we want to tell everybody about it. That's why we talk so much to one another. Even when we are by ourselves, we have the need to share our story, and we share it with ourselves. We see a beautiful sunset and we say, "Oh, what a beautiful sunset!" Nobody is listening except us, but we talk to ourselves anyway.

We also have the need to know other people's stories because we like to compare notes, or we can say that as artists we like to compare our art. We see a movie, we like it, and we ask the friend who went with us, "What did you think about the movie?" Well, maybe our friend has another point of view and tells us things about the movie that we didn't see. Very soon we change our mind and say, "Well, that movie was not as good as I thought it was." We are constantly exchanging information and modifying our story in this way. This is how the dream of humanity evolves. Our personal dream mixes with the dream of other dreamers, and this modifies the bigger dream of society.

You are dreaming the story of your life, and I can assure you that it's an art. Your art is the art of creating stories and sharing stories. If I met you today, I would see the real you behind your story. I would see you as the force of life creating art through you. Your story could be the best screenplay for any movie because all of us are professional storytellers. But I know that whatever you tell me is just a story. I don't have to believe your story, but I can listen to your story and enjoy it. I can go to the movies to see *The Godfather*, and I don't believe it, but I can enjoy it, right?

What I'm sharing with you is my personal process about how I recovered my personal freedom. I am grateful for the opportunity to share my story, but it's just a story, and it's only true for me. Something I find very interesting is that every time I share this story it is different. I try to distort it as little as possible, but even my own story changes. Despite the distortion, if you can understand it, you can compare it to your own art.

Many times we don't see our own creation; we don't see our own lies. But sometimes in the reflection of somebody else, we can see our own magnificence. By experiencing the love of another person, we can see how great we are. From one artist to another artist, we might see that it's possible to improve our own art.

Once we have the awareness to see our own story, we discover there is another way of creating the main character. Without awareness, there is nothing we can do, because the story is so powerful that the story writes itself. We create the story, we give our personal power to the story, and then the story is living our lives. But with awareness, we recover the control of our story. That is the good news. If we don't like our story, we are the authors; we can change it.

❧

POINTS TO PONDER

• You are the author of an ongoing story you tell yourself. In your story, everything is about you, and it has to be that way because you are the center of your perception. The story is told from your point of view.

• You create an image for the secondary characters in your story, and you assign them a role to play. The only thing you know about the secondary characters is the story you create about them. The truth is that you don't know anyone, and nobody knows you either.

• Respect is one of the greatest expressions of love. If other people try to write your story, it means they don't respect you. They consider that you are not a good artist who can write your own story, even though you were born to write your own story.

• The only way to change your story is to change what you believe about yourself. If you clean up the lies you believe about yourself, the lies you believe about everybody else will change. Every time you change the main character of your story, the whole story changes to adapt to the new main character.

• Don't waste your time taking anything personally. When other people talk to you, they are really talking to the secondary character in their story. Whatever people say about you is just a projection of their *image* of you. It has nothing to do with you.

• Humans are the storytellers of God. It is our nature to make up stories, to interpret everything we perceive. Without awareness, we give our personal power to the story, and the story writes itself. With awareness, we recover the control of our story. We see that we are the authors, and if we don't like our story, we change it.

6

Inner Peace

Taming the voice with two rules

More and more, I kept exploring the whole dynamic of the story that humans create. What I discovered is that the story has a voice — a voice so loud, yet only we can hear it. As I said before, you can call it *thinking* if you want; I call it *the voice of knowledge*. That voice is always there. It never stops. It's not even real, but we hear it. Of course you can say, "Well, it's me. I'm the one who is talking." But if you are the voice that is talking, then who is listening?

The voice of knowledge can also be called *the liar who lives in your head.* A beautiful Tree of Knowledge lives in your head, and it's the home for guess who? The Prince of Lies. Oh yes, and this is the problem because the voice of the liar speaks in your language, but your integrity, your spirit, the truth, has no language. You just know truth; you feel it. The voice of your spirit tries to come out, but the voice of the liar is stronger and louder and it hooks your attention almost all of the time.

You hear the voice — and not just one voice, but an entire *mitote*, which is like a thousand voices talking all at once. And what are these voices telling you? "Look at you. Who do you think you are? You will never make it. You aren't smart enough. Why should I try? Nobody understands me. What is he doing? What is she doing? What if he doesn't love me? I'm so lonely. Nobody wants to be with me. Nobody really likes me. I wonder if those people are talking about me. What will they think about me? Look at all the injustice in the world. How can I be happy when millions of people are dying of starvation?"

The voice of knowledge is telling you what you are and what you are not. It's always trying to make sense out of everything. I call it *the voice of knowledge* because it's telling you everything you know. It's telling you your point of view in a conversation that never ends. For many people it's even worse because the voice is not just talking nonsense; the voice is judging and criticizing. It's constantly gossiping in your head about you and the people around you.

That voice is usually lying because it's the voice of what you have learned, and you have learned so many lies, mainly about yourself. You cannot see the liar, but you can hear the voice. The voice of knowledge can come from your own head, or it can come from people around you. It can be your own opinion, or it can be the opinion of somebody else, but your emotional reaction to that voice is telling you, "I'm being abused."

Every time we judge ourselves, find ourselves guilty, and punish ourselves, it's because the voice in our head is telling us lies. Every time we have a conflict with our father, our mother, our children, or our beloved, it's because we believe in these lies, and they believe in them, too. But it's not just that. When we believe in lies, we cannot see the truth, so we make thousands of assumptions and we take them as truth.

One of the biggest assumptions we make is that the lies we believe are the truth! For example, we believe that we know what we are. When we get angry we say, "Oh, that's the way I am." When we get jealous: "Oh, that's the way I am." When we hate: "Oh, that's the way I am." But is this true? I'm not sure about that. I used to make the assumption that I was the one who was talking, that I was the one who said all of those things that I didn't want to say. It was a big surprise when I discovered that it was not me; it was the way I learned to be. And I practiced and practiced until I mastered that performance.

The voice that says, "That's the way I am," is the voice of knowledge. It's the voice of the liar living in the Tree of Knowledge in your head. The Toltec consider it a mental disease that is highly contagious because it's transmitted from human to human through knowledge. The symptoms of the disease are fear, anger, hatred, sadness, jealousy, conflict, and separation between humans. Again, these lies are controlling the dream of our life. I think this is obvious.

My grandfather told me in the simplest way, "Miguel, the conflict is between the truth and what is not the truth," and this was nothing new. Two thousand years ago one of the greatest masters, at least in my story, said, "And you will know the truth, and the truth will set you free." Free from what? From all those lies. Especially from the liar who lives in your head and talks to you all the time. And we call it *thinking!* I used to tell my apprentices, "Just because you hear a voice in your head it doesn't mean that it's speaking the truth. Well, don't believe that voice, and that voice won't have any power over you."

There is a movie that illustrates my point beautifully. It's called *A Beautiful Mind*. At first I thought, "Oh, another spy movie," but I became more interested when I realized that the main character is schizophrenic. He is a brilliant man, a genius, but he sees people who don't exist. These people are controlling his life because he listens to their opinions and follows whatever they tell him to do. They are lying to him, and by listening to what they tell him, he is ruining his life. He has no idea that these people are hallucinations until his wife puts him in a mental hospital, where he is diagnosed as schizophrenic and given medication. The visions disappear, but the drug has secondary effects, and he decides to stop taking it. Without the drug, the visions come back, and he finds out that it's true that nobody else can see the people he sees. Now he has to make a choice: go back to the hospital, lose his wife, and accept that he is mentally ill, or face the visions and overcome them.

When he finally has the awareness that the people he sees are not real, he makes a very smart decision. He says, "I will not pay attention to them. I will not believe what they tell me." The power the visions have over him is lost when he no longer believes in them. With this awareness, he finds peace, and after many years of not putting his attention on them, the visions hardly talk to him anymore. Even though he still sees them, they don't waste their time because he doesn't listen to them anyway.

This movie is wonderful because it shows that if you don't believe the voice in your head, it loses the power it has over you, and you become authentic again. The voice in your head isn't even real, but it's ruling your life, and it's a tyrant. Once that voice hooks your attention, it makes you do whatever it wants you to do.

How many times has the voice made you say *yes* when you really wanted to say *no*? Or the opposite —the voice made you say *no* when you really wanted to say *yes*? How many times has the voice made you doubt what you feel in your heart? How many times have you missed opportunities to do what you really want to do in your life because of fear — fear that was a reaction to believing the voice in your head? How many times have you broken up with someone you really loved just because the voice of knowledge told you to do it? How many times have you tried to control the people you love because you follow that voice? How many times have you gotten angry or jealous or lost control and hurt the people you really love just because you believed that voice?

You can see what you have done by following instructions from the voice of knowledge — by following the lies. That voice tells you so many things to do that go against yourself, just like the visions of the character in the movie. The only difference between you and that man is that maybe you don't see the visions, but you hear the voice. It's overwhelming, it never stops, and we pretend that we are mentally sane!

It is obvious that the voice of knowledge is the story talking by itself. As soon as an idea hooks your attention, your story goes in that direction. Then it takes you anywhere and everywhere without any direction. Every idea is repeating itself, and there are so many ideas in your head competing for your attention that the voice is changing from one moment to the next — boom, boom, boom!

I compare the voice of knowledge to a wild horse that is taking you wherever it wants to go. You have no control over that horse. But if you cannot *stop* the horse, at least you can try to *tame* the horse. I tell my apprentices, "Once you learn to tame the horse, you will ride the horse, and thinking becomes a tool that takes you where *you* want to go. If you don't believe that voice, it becomes quieter and quieter, and speaks to you less and less until it stops talking to you."

If you have to talk to yourself, then why not be friendly? Why not tell yourself how beautiful and wonderful you are? Then at least you have someone to talk to when you're alone. But if the voice in your head is nasty and abusive, then it's no fun at all. If that voice is telling you lies, if it's letting you know why you should be ashamed of yourself or why your beloved doesn't love you, then it's better to be quiet.

If you don't like a person, you can walk away from that person. If you don't like yourself, you can't escape yourself; you are with yourself wherever you go. This is why some people try to numb themselves with alcohol or drugs. Or maybe they overeat or gamble to make themselves forget who they are with. Of course this doesn't work because the storyteller judges everything we do, and this only leads to more shame and self-rejection.

Long ago I stopped listening to the voice of knowledge. I remember that I used to go outside and tell myself, "Oh, look at the beautiful clouds, the flowers, mmm, they smell so good" — as if I didn't know that! I no longer make up stories for myself. I know what I know. Why tell myself what I already know? Does that make sense? It's just a habit. I don't waste my time and energy by talking to myself. I no longer have that ongoing voice in my head, and I can assure you that it's wonderful.

You don't need internal dialogue; you can know without thinking. The value of cultivating a silent mind has been known for thousands of years. In India, people use meditation and the chanting of mantras to stop the internal dialogue. To have peace in your head is incredible. Imagine being in an environment where there is a constant sound — bzzzz, bzzzz, bzzzz. The moment comes when you don't even notice the noise. You know something is bothering you, but you no longer notice what it is. The moment the noise stops, you notice the silence and feel the relief, "Ahhh..." When the voice in your head finally stops talking, it feels something like that. I call it *inner peace.*

When I shared this with my apprentices, they understood what I was telling them. They said, "We know the voice of knowledge lives in our head, and we know that it's a liar, but how do we stop it from talking to us? Can you give us a little more help?" By that time, I had already won over the voice, and I was completely at peace. I said, "Okay, I will give you two simple rules. If you follow these rules, there is a chance that you will tame the voice or even win the challenge against the liar."

The solution for taming the liar is to *stop believing* what it tells you. What happens when someone tells you a lie, and you know it's a lie? It doesn't affect you because you don't *believe* the lie. If you don't believe it, the lie cannot survive the test of your skepticism, and boom! The lie disappears. Simple. But in that simplicity there is also a big challenge. Why? Because believing your own lies makes you feel safe, and believing the lies of other people is very tempting. When you are ready for the challenge, the following two rules will accelerate the process of purifying your belief system, which is everything in your personal Tree of Knowledge.

Rule number one: *Don't believe yourself.* But keep your mind open. Keep your heart open. Listen to yourself, listen to your story, but don't *believe* it because now you know that the story you are writing is fiction. It's not real. When you hear the voice in your head, don't take it personally. You know that knowledge is usually lying to you. Listen, and ask if it's speaking the truth or not. If you don't believe your own lies, your lies will not survive, and you can make better choices based on truth.

Don't believe yourself, but learn to listen because sometimes the voice of knowledge can have a brilliant idea, and if you agree with the idea, then take it. It could be a moment of inspiration that leads to a great opportunity in life. Respect your story, and learn to *really* listen. When you listen to your story, the communication with yourself will improve 100 percent. You will see your story with clarity, and if you don't like the story, you can change it.

Don't believe yourself mainly when you are using the voice against yourself. The voice can make you afraid to be alive, to express who you really are. It can stop you from doing what you really want to do with your life. That voice has been in control of your head for so many years, and, no, that voice will not give up just because you want it to leave you alone. But at least you can challenge that voice by not believing what it's telling you. That's why I say, "Don't believe yourself."

Rule number two: *Don't believe anybody else.* And that includes me for the same reason. You know that if you lie to yourself, surely other people lie to themselves. And if they lie to themselves, surely they will lie to you as well. When people talk to you, who is speaking through them? Who is dictating what they say? You have no idea if what they are saying is coming from their heart or from the Prince of Lies who lives in their head. You don't know, so don't believe them. But learn to listen without judging. You don't need to judge people because they lie. How many times have you heard someone say, "Oh, he's a pathological liar," when in reality everybody is possessed by the Prince of Lies? There are lies everywhere. People are always lying, and when they don't have awareness, they don't even know it. Sometimes they really believe that what they are saying is true. And they can really *believe* it, but it doesn't mean that it's true.

Don't believe anybody, but this doesn't mean closing your mind or your heart. Listen to other people tell their story. You know that it's just a story, and that it's only true for them. When you listen, you can understand their story; you can see where people are coming from, and the communication can be wonderful. Other people need to express their story, to project what they believe, but you don't have to agree with what they say. *Don't believe,* but learn to listen. Even if it's just a story, sometimes the words that come from other storytellers come from their integrity. When this happens, your own integrity recognizes it right away, and you agree with what they are saying. Their voice goes directly to your spirit, and you feel you already know that what they are telling you is the truth.

Don't believe anybody else, but listen because sometimes a moment of inspiration or opportunity can come through the voice of someone else. The way other people create their story might reflect the way you create your story, and when they are exposed, you can see how they invest their faith in lies. You might see the lies right away, when you couldn't see them in yourself. By listening to their story, you might recognize the truth about something you do all the time, and that truth can change your own story. Listen to their story, but *don't believe it.* That is the key.

If other people tell you, "Look at the way you are dressed!" that remark doesn't ruin your day. You listen to their story, but you *don't believe it.* You can decide if it's true or not according to your story, but you don't have an emotional reaction anymore. If you decide that it's true, you can change what you are wearing, and there's no more problem. This is something simple that is happening all the time. People constantly express their point of view, and we may even ask for their point of view, but *don't believe them!*

When people talk about you, now you know they are talking about a secondary character in their story who represents you. They are talking about an *image* they create for you. You know that it has nothing to do with you. But if you agree, if you *believe* what they say, then their story becomes a part of your story. If you take it personally, it modifies your story. If you don't take it personally, the opinions of others do not affect you the way they used to, and you have more patience with people. This helps you to avoid a great deal of conflict.

If you follow these two rules — *don't believe yourself*, and *don't believe anybody else* — all of the lies that come from the voice of knowledge won't survive your skepticism. Being skeptical is not about being judgmental; it is not about taking the position that you are more intelligent than others. You just don't believe, and what is true will become obvious. This is very interesting because the truth survives your skepticism even if you don't believe it. That is the beauty of the truth. The truth doesn't need anybody to believe it. The truth is still the truth whether or not you believe it. Can we say the same about lies? No, lies only exist because we believe them. If we don't believe in lies, they simply disappear.

Every day the sun is in the sky whether we believe it or not. The Earth is round, even if the entire world believes that it's flat. Hundreds of years ago, everyone believed this lie. They would swear that the Earth was flat, and they were certain that the Earth was the center of the universe, with the sun revolving around it. People really believed this; they had no doubt about it. But just because they believed it, did that make it true? No, but believing those lies made them feel safe.

Humans believe so many lies. Some of these lies are so subtle and convincing that we base our entire virtual reality on them without even noticing that they are lies. The lies we believe about ourselves can be difficult to see because we are so used to them that they seem normal.

For example, if you believe the common lie

"I'm not worth it," that lie lives in your mind because you believe it. You don't believe people who tell you how great you are, and you don't believe them because you believe the opposite. Your faith is already invested in a belief that is not the truth; it's a lie, but your faith guides your actions. By not feeling worthy, how do you express yourself with other people? You are shy. How can you ask for something when you do not believe you are worth it? What you believe about yourself is what you project to other people, and that is what others then believe about you. Of course, that is how they treat you, which only reinforces the belief that you aren't worth it. And what is the truth? The truth is that you are worth it; everybody is worth it.

If you believe the lie that you cannot speak in public then *thy will be done:* When you try to speak in public, you are afraid. The only way to break your faith in this agreement is by taking the action and doing it. Then you prove that it's a lie, and you are no longer afraid.

If you believe that you cannot have a loving relationship, *thy will be done*. If you feel that you don't deserve love, even if love is in front of you, you just don't take it because you are blind to it. You only see what you want to see, and you only hear what you want to hear. Everything you perceive is just more support for your lies.

If you understand these examples, you can just imagine how many lies you believe about yourself, and how many lies you believe about your parents, your children, your siblings, or your partner. Every time you judge them, you give voice to the false beliefs in your own Tree of Knowledge. You give your power to these lies, and what is the result? Anger or jealousy or even hate. Then you accumulate all of that emotional poison, and the moment comes when you lose control and say something that you don't want to say.

Can you see the power of what I'm sharing with you? You can change your life by refusing to believe your own lies. You can start with the main lies that limit the expression of your happiness and your love. If you take your faith away from these lies, they lose their power over you. Then you can recover your faith and invest it in different beliefs. If you stop believing in lies, everything in your life changes, just like magic.

There is a part of *The Iliad* by Homer that I really love: "We, the gods, will live as long as the humans believe in us. The day the humans no longer believe in us, all the gods will disappear." This is beautiful. Centuries ago, the Greek gods were worshiped by hundreds of thousands of people; today, they are just legends. When we don't believe in lies, the lies disappear, and the truth becomes obvious.

Many lies enslave us, but only one thing can free us, and it's the truth. Only the truth can set us free from the fear, the drama, and the conflict in our lives. This is the absolute truth, and I cannot put it more simply than that.

POINTS TO PONDER

• What you call *thinking* is the voice of knowledge making up stories, telling you what you know, and trying to make sense out of everything you don't know. The problem is that the voice makes you do many things that go against yourself.

• The voice in your head is like a wild horse taking you wherever *it* wants to go. Once you tame the horse, you can ride the horse, and knowledge becomes a tool for communication that takes you where *you* want to go.

• You don't need internal dialogue; you can know without thinking. You can perceive with your feelings. Why waste energy telling yourself what you already know or worrying about what you don't know? When the voice in your head finally stops talking, you experience *inner peace*.

• The solution for taming the liar in your head is to *stop believing* what it tells you. If you follow two rules — *don't believe yourself*, and *don't believe anybody else* — all of the lies you believe won't survive your skepticism and will simply disappear.

• The truth survives our skepticism, but we cannot say the same about lies. Lies can only survive if we believe them. The truth is still the truth, whether or not we believe it. That is the beauty of the truth.

• The voice of knowledge rules your life, and it is a tyrant. If you refuse to obey that voice, it becomes quieter and quieter, and speaks to you less and less until it no longer controls you. When the voice loses power over you, lies no longer rule your life, and you become authentic again.

7

EMOTIONS ARE REAL

The voice of knowledge is not real

BEFORE YOU LEARN TO SPEAK, YOUR BRAIN IS LIKE a perfect computer, but without a program. When you are born, you don't know a language. It takes several years for your brain to mature enough to receive a program. Then the program is introduced to you, mainly through your parents, as well as other people around you. They hook your attention and teach you the meaning of words. You learn to speak, and the program goes inside you little by little by agreement. You agree, and now you have the program.

Well, if you are the computer, then knowledge is the program. Everything you know, all of the knowledge in your head, was already in the program before you were born. I can assure you that none of us ever has an original idea. Every letter, every word, every concept in your belief system is part of the program, and that program is contaminated with a virus called *lies*.

There's no need to judge the program as good or bad or right or wrong. Even if we don't like the program, nobody is guilty for sharing it with us. It's just the way it is, and it's wonderful because we use the program to create our stories. But who is running our life? The program! The program has a voice, and it's lying to us all the time.

How can we know what the truth is when almost everything we have learned is a lie? How can we recognize what is real in us? Well, it took some time for me to find out, but I found out. Our emotions are real. Every emotion that we feel is real, it is truth, *it is*. I discovered that every emotion comes directly from our spirit, from our integrity; it is completely authentic.

You cannot fake what you feel. You can try to repress your emotions, you can try to justify what you feel or lie about what you feel, but what you feel is authentic. It is real, and you are feeling it. There is nothing wrong with whatever you feel. There are no good emotions or bad emotions; there is nothing wrong with anger or jealousy or envy. Even if you are feeling hate, it comes from your integrity. Even if it's sadness or depression that you are suffering, if you feel it, there is always a reason for feeling it.

I discovered something very interesting about the human mind, something logical and important to understand. Everything you perceive causes an emotional reaction — *everything*. If you perceive beauty, your emotional reaction is wonderful; you feel great. When you are hurt, your emotional reaction is not so great. But you perceive not just the outside world;

you perceive the virtual world you create in your head. You perceive not only your feelings, but your knowledge — your own thoughts, judgments, and beliefs. You perceive the voice in your head, and you have an emotional reaction to that voice.

Now the question is this: What is the voice in your head telling you? How many times has it told you, "God, I'm so stupid, how could I do that? I will never learn!" The voice of knowledge judges you, you perceive the judgment, and you have an emotional reaction. You feel the shame; you feel the guilt. The emotion is true, but what causes the emotion, which is the judgment that you are stupid, is not true; it's a story. Again, this is just action–reaction. What is the action? The action is the perception of your point of view, which means the perception of your own judgment. What is the reaction? Your feelings are the reaction, and you react to the lies with emotional poison.

Let's see if we can understand this a little better. Imagine that you have a dog. As you know, the dog is just a dog, and it's a perfect dog, isn't it? But what happens if you abuse the dog? What if every time you see the dog, you kick the dog? Very soon the dog will be afraid. You can see the emotions coming from the dog. It is angry; it might try to bite you or run away. Is there something wrong with the dog's emotions? Does the dog's anger make the dog evil? No, the dog's reaction is just the result of being abused. The emotion is helping the dog to defend itself. It comes from the dog's integrity.

Now imagine a dog living in the most beautiful environment with people who always love and respect the dog. That dog is the sweetest animal in the whole world, the most wonderful dog. Because that dog is not abused, he follows his nature; he loves everybody who loves him. Well, your physical body is just like that dog. It reacts emotionally in the same way. Why do you react with anger? Well, because somebody kicked you, right? But who kicked you? The voice in your head, the main character of your story — what you *believe* you are.

You also perceive your image of perfection, what you believe you *are not*, and this also creates an emotional reaction. How do you feel when you cannot live up to that image? The emotion is not pleasant, but your emotional reaction is real; it's what you feel. But is it true that you need to fit that image? No, it's a lie. What you are perceiving is just a lie that you agreed to believe in. You agreed, and that lie has become a part of your story.

Humans are victimized by knowledge, by what we *know*. If we make a mistake in front of someone, we try to justify the mistake to protect the image we project. Later, when we are alone, we remember what happened, and we punish ourselves all over again. Why? Because the voice of knowledge keeps telling us what we did from the same point of view that we had when we did it. The voice becomes a powerful judge, and it's telling us, "Look what you did!" And it's telling this to whom? It was the voice that made us do it in the first place!

The voice of knowledge is abusing the emotional body. What is not real is abusing what is real. The action is to believe a lie; the reaction is to feel emotional pain. The emotional body perceives the voice, reacts to the voice, and just like a tiger, it attacks. We lose control, and we do things and say things that we really don't want to do or say. Now the voice of knowledge is afraid of our emotional reaction; it judges our reaction, and makes us feel ashamed of our own feelings.

Then we perceive the emotion of shame, and use knowledge to try to justify the emotion, which means the voice of knowledge is talking about what we feel. The voice starts lying about our feelings, and even tries to deny what we feel. Then we perceive that voice, we perceive the judgment, and we have another emotional reaction. Now we feel guilty because we reacted emotionally. Then knowledge tries to explain the emotion of guilt. The emotional pain is growing, and now we are depressed. Can you see the cycle?

The voice of knowledge makes a story about our emotions, we perceive the story, and we try to repress our emotions. Perceiving that repression creates another emotional reaction, and soon we just want to repress everything we feel. "I shouldn't feel this way. What kind of man are you? Are you a wimp or what? Real men don't cry." We pretend it doesn't hurt. Yes it hurts, but it hurts because we make a story, perceive the story, and drag more emotions into the story.

Why do we hate? Because someone is abusing us. That's why we hate. Why do we suffer? Because something is hurting us. That's why we suffer. It's a normal reaction to being hurt. But what is hurting us? Well, now the answer is easy. What hurts us is the voice of the liar in our head that keeps telling us the way we *should* be, but we *are not*. The hate, the anger, and the jealousy are normal emotional reactions that come from what is real, which means they come from our integrity, not from who we are pretending to be.

That's why there is nothing wrong with hate. If we feel hate, the voice of knowledge speaking in our head is causing us to hate. The hate is completely normal; it's just a reaction to what we believe. If we change the belief, then the hate will transform into love. All of our emotions change when we no longer believe the voice because the emotions are the effect, not the cause. Emotional pain is a symptom of being abused; the pain is letting us know that we have to do something to stop the abuse.

Why do people abuse us? Because we allow them to abuse us, because in our judgment we believe we deserve to be abused. But if we go a little deeper, we see that we abuse ourselves far more than anybody else abuses us. We can blame other people who hurt us and say, "I grew up being abused," and we can make many excuses. But in the present moment, who is abusing you? If you are truthful, you find that mostly it's your own voice of knowledge.

Every time we lie to ourselves, we abuse ourselves. Every time we curse ourselves, we abuse ourselves. Every time we judge ourselves, every time we reject ourselves, of course we have an emotional reaction, and it isn't pleasant! Again, if we don't like the emotional reaction, it's not about repressing what we feel; it's about cleaning up the lies that cause the emotional reaction.

The message coming from our integrity is clear. The voice of integrity is screaming to us, "Please, save me!" That reminds me of the movie *The Exorcist*, about a little girl who is possessed by demons. Well, there is a little girl inside us saying, "Help me! I'm being possessed by the main character of my story!" Oh, my goodness — and it's true! Humans are possessed by knowledge. We are possessed by a distorted image of ourselves, and that is why we are no longer free. How many times have you heard someone say, "If the real me comes out, I don't know what's going to happen"? We are afraid that something inside of us will come out and destroy everything. And you know what? It is true. If the real you comes out, it will destroy all of the lies, and that *is* frightening.

I used to be possessed by the main character of my story. I was abused by that character for so many years, yet I pretended to love myself. What a joke! And not just that, I pretended to love somebody else. How could I love somebody else when I didn't love myself? I can only give to others what I have for myself.

People have asked me, "Miguel, why can't I feel love? How can I learn to create love?" I thought about this. Hmm . . . Create love? Then a little idea came into my mind. We don't need to learn how to love. By nature, we love. Before we learn to speak, love is the main emotion we feel. It is natural to express our love, but then we learn to repress our love. And I tell them, "You don't need to create love. Your heart is made to produce so much love that you can send your love to the entire world. If you can't feel love, it's because you are resisting love; it's because you've learned how to stop expressing your love."

When we are little children and people tell us that we shouldn't be the way we are, we begin to repress the expression of our authentic self. We repress our integrity, our own emotional body. We practice hiding our emotions and pretending that we don't feel them. When we feel ashamed of our emotions, we begin to justify and explain and judge our emotions. We believe in so many lies that we no longer express the beautiful emotion of love.

The voice of knowledge tells us, "It's not safe to love. I'm afraid to love because love makes me vulnerable. If I love, my heart will be broken." So many lies. It's not the truth, but knowledge tells you, "Of course it's true. I have a lot of experience with this. Every time I love, my heart is broken." Well, this isn't the truth because nobody can break your heart if you love yourself. If your heart was broken in the past, you broke it with the lies you believed about love. Love makes you strong; selfishness makes you weak. Love doesn't hurt. What hurts is the fear, selfishness, and control that come from the lies you believe in. If you no longer believe in lies, automatically love starts coming out of you.

After my experience in the desert, it was clear to me that every emotion I feel comes directly from my integrity. When I noticed this, I no longer repressed my emotions. Now my emotions are the most important part of my story because I know that my feelings are authentic. When I feel an emotion, I know it's a reaction to what I perceive. My emotions are telling me how I am doing in my life, and by following my emotions, I can change my circumstances.

Whatever the feeling — from joy to anger, from love to hate — it is just a reaction. But being a reaction, it is important to see the action. If I am not happy, it's because there is something in my story that is suppressing my happiness. Then I have to take a step back and see what is causing it. If I have the awareness, I can face the problem, fix the problem, and be happy again. As soon as any problem arises in my life, I resolve it in one way or another without even trying to make a story about it.

The universe is simple: it's about cause and effect, action and reaction. If you don't like the way you are living your life, this is a reaction to the program that is ruling your life. The liar, the program, is not even part of you, but at the same time, it *is* part of you because it's the way you identify yourself. The program creates the story, then it tries to make sense of the story by explaining and justifying everything to the main character of the story. What a setup. What a creation. Humans create an entire culture, a whole philosophy of humanity. We create history, science, art, Olympic games, Miss Universe, you name it. It's our creation, and it's beautiful and wonderful, but it's just a *story!*

The main character of your story is you, but the role that you are playing is not you. You have practiced that role for so long that you have mastered the performance. You have become the best actor in the entire world, but I can assure you that you are not what you believe you are. Thank God, because you are much better than what you believe you are.

I remember when my Grandfather told me, "Miguel, you will know that you are free when you no longer have to be you." At that moment, I didn't understand him, but later I knew exactly what he meant. I don't have to be the way everybody wants me to be. I don't have to be what I believe *I should be* according to my own lies.

Your story is your creation. You are the artist with the force of life flowing through you. If you don't like your art, you have the power to change it. That's the good news. You don't have to be you anymore, and that's the maximum freedom. You don't have to be what you *believe* you are. You don't have to be that anger or that jealousy or that hate. You can recover the sense of what you really are, return to paradise, and live again in heaven on earth.

❦

Points to Ponder

• Every emotion that you feel is real. It is truth. It comes directly from the integrity of your spirit. You cannot fake what you feel. You can try to justify or repress your emotions, you can try to lie about what you feel, but what you feel is authentic.

• The voice of knowledge can make you feel ashamed of your feelings, but there is nothing wrong with whatever you feel. There are no good emotions or bad emotions. Even if what you feel is anger or hate, it comes from your integrity. If you feel it, there is always a reason for feeling it.

• Everything you perceive causes an emotional reaction. You perceive not only your feelings, but your knowledge

— your own thoughts, judgments, and beliefs. You perceive the voice in your head, and you have an emotional reaction to that voice.

• Every time you lie to yourself, or judge yourself, or reject yourself, you have an emotional reaction, and it isn't pleasant. If you don't like the emotional reaction, it's not about repressing what you feel; it's about cleaning up the lies that cause it. All of your emotions change when you no longer believe in lies because the emotions are the effect, not the cause.

• Our emotions are real; the voice of knowledge that makes us suffer is not. Our suffering is true, but the reason why we suffer may not be true at all.

• Humans are possessed by knowledge, by a distorted image of ourselves. That is why we are no longer free.

• Emotional pain is a symptom of being abused; the pain is letting you know that you have to do something to stop the abuse. The emotions are the most important part of your story because they are telling you how you are doing in your life. By following your emotions, you can change your circumstances.

8

COMMON SENSE AND BLIND FAITH

Recovering our faith and free will

WHEN I STARTED TEACHING THIS PHILOSOPHY, one of my challenges was to share the wisdom of my tradition without the superstition. I wanted to take away all of the superstition, all of the things about evil and witchcraft from the Toltec tradition. Who cares about all the lies? I wanted to take away the nonsense, and only keep the common sense.

If we take away the superstition and mythology from the traditions around the world, the result is pure common sense. When it comes to common sense, there is no difference between the Toltec tradition, the Egyptian tradition, the Christian tradition, the Buddhist tradition, the Islamic tradition, or any other tradition, because all of these philosophies come from the same place. They come directly from human integrity.

The difference is in the story. Each philosophy has tried to explain with symbols something that is so difficult to say with words. The masters witnessed the truth and created a story, depending on what they believed. The story became mythology, and the people who were not masters created all of the superstition and lies. That is why I don't believe in following gurus or idolizing heroes. We are our own gurus, our own heroes. What I am sharing with you is the way I live my life, but I'm not telling you how to live your life. It's not my business; it's your business. But seeing the way that I dream can give you an idea of what you can do with your dream.

As you read this book, perhaps you will feel as if you are reading something you already know: your own common sense. In one moment, you can return to your common sense, to your own integrity. You can have clarity again, and see what others cannot see. You can live with awareness and recover a wonderful power that humans gave up long ago: faith.

Faith is a force that comes from our integrity. It is the expression of what we really are. Faith is the power of our creation because we use faith to create our life story and to transform our life story. Different traditions have called this power by different names. The Toltec call it *intent*, but I prefer to call it *faith*.

Let's see if we can understand why our faith is so important. When we talk about faith or intent, we are also talking about the power of the word. The word is pure magic. It is a power that comes directly from God, and faith is the force that directs this power. We can say that everything in our virtual reality is created with the word because we use the word for the creation of our story. Humans have the most wonderful imagination. Beginning with the word, we form a language. With a language, we try to make sense out of everything we experience.

First we agree about the sound and meaning of each word. Then just by remembering the sound of the words, we can communicate with other dreamers about our virtual reality. We give names to everything we perceive; we choose words as symbols, and these symbols have the power to reproduce a dream in our head. For example, just hearing the word *horse* can reproduce an entire image in our mind. That's how a symbol works. But it can even be more powerful than that. Just by saying two words, "*The Godfather,*" a whole movie can appear in our mind. The word, as a symbol, has the magic and power of creation because it can reproduce an image, a concept, or an entire situation in our imagination.

It is amazing what the word can do. The word creates images of objects in our mind. The word creates complex concepts. The word evokes feelings.

The word creates every belief that we store in our mind. The structure of our language shapes how we perceive our entire virtual reality.

Faith is so important because it is the force that gives life to every word, to every concept that we store in our mind. We can say that life manifests through faith, and that faith is a messenger of life. Life goes through our faith, and then our faith gives life to everything we agree to believe in. Remember, we invest our faith by making an agreement. When we agree with a concept, we accept the concept without any doubt, and the concept becomes a part of us. If we don't agree with a concept, our faith is not there, and we don't keep it in our memory. Every concept is alive just because our faith is there, just because we *believe* in the concept. Faith is the force that holds all of these symbols together and gives sense and direction to the entire dream.

If you can imagine that every belief, every concept, every opinion is like a brick, then our faith is the mortar that holds the bricks together. The way we start getting these bricks and putting them together is by using our attention. Humans can perceive millions of things simultaneously, but with our attention we have the power to discriminate and focus only on what we want to perceive. The attention is also the part of our mind that we use to transfer information from person to person. By hooking someone's attention, we create a channel of communication, and through that channel we can send and receive information. This is how we teach, and this is how we learn.

As I have said, our parents hook our attention and teach us the meaning of words; we agree, and we learn a language. Through language, the word, we start to build the edifice of knowledge. Together, all of our beliefs form a structure that tells us what we believe we are. The Toltec call this shape that our mind takes *the human form*. The human form is not the form of our physical body. The human form is the structure of our personal Tree of Knowledge. It is everything we believe about being a human; it is the structure of our whole story. This structure is almost as solid as our physical body because our faith makes it rigid.

You call yourself a human, and that is what makes you a human. Your faith is invested in your story — mostly in the main character of your story — and that is the main problem! The most powerful part of you, your faith, is invested in the liar who lives in your head. Through your faith, you give life to all of those lies. The result is the way you live your life in the present moment because you have faith in the main character of your story. This means that you believe in what you believe you are without any doubt. The rest is just action–reaction. Every habit is a setup for you to perform the role of your main character.

The storyteller has power over you because you have faith in the story that it tells you. Once you support the story with your faith, it doesn't matter whether the story is the truth or not the truth. You believe it; you are done. *Thy will be done.* That is why Jesus said that if you have just a little faith you can move mountains. Humans are powerful because we have a strong faith; we have the capacity to believe strongly, but where is our faith invested? Why do we feel that we have hardly any faith? I can tell you that it's not true that we have so little faith. Our faith is strong and powerful, but our faith is not free. Our faith is invested in all of the knowledge in our head. It is trapped in the structure of our Tree of Knowledge.

The structure is what really controls the dream of our life because our faith lives in that structure. Our faith is not in the voice of our story, and it's not in our reasoning mind. Just because we say, "I will succeed," doesn't mean that our faith follows those words. No, there may be another belief that is stronger and deeper, and that belief is telling us, "You will not succeed." And that is what happens. It doesn't matter what we do; we fail.

That is why you cannot change yourself just by wishing to change. No, you need to really challenge what you believe you are, especially the beliefs that limit the expression of your life. You need to challenge every belief that you use to judge yourself, to reject yourself, to make yourself little.

I remember one of my apprentices asking me, "Miguel, why is it so difficult to change my beliefs?" And I told him, "Well, you understand the concept that what you believe you are is not the truth; it's a story. You understand that very well, but you don't *believe* it. And that is what makes the difference. If you really believe it, if your faith is there, then you change."

So yes, it is possible to change what we believe, to recreate the dream of our life, but first we need to free our faith. And there is only one way to free our faith, and that way is through the truth. The truth is our sword, and it's the only weapon we have against the lies. Nothing but the truth can free the faith that is trapped in the structure of our lies. But with our faith invested in the lies, we no longer see the truth. The lies blind our faith, the power of our creation.

Blind faith is a powerful concept. When our faith is blind, we no longer follow the truth. That is what happened when we ate the fruit of the Tree of Knowledge. We believed the lies, our faith was blinded, and we followed an illusion that was not true. God told us, "You may die." And our faith in lies is death because we lose our power of creation, which is our connection with life or God. We fall into the illusion that we are separate from life, and this leads to self-destruction and death.

If your faith is blind, it is leading you nowhere. That is why Jesus said if the blind lead the blind, both fall. Now you know why other people's stories do not really help you; it is just like the blind lead-ing the blind. If you have blind faith and you teach blind faith, both fall. If you believe that life is against you, and you teach that life is against you, both are blind because you don't see the truth. Now both believe the lie!

Real faith, or free faith, is what you are feeling in this moment. This moment is real; you have faith in life, faith in yourself, faith for no reason. This is the power of your creation in the moment. From that point of power, you can create whatever you want to create in any direction.

Blind faith is faith without awareness, but when your faith has awareness, that's a different story. When your faith has awareness, you never use the power of your faith against yourself, which means you are impeccable with your word. When you are impeccable with your word, your entire life improves in every direction. Why? Because the impeccability of your word goes directly to the main character of your story, where most of your faith is invested. To be impeccable with your word means that you never use the word against yourself in the creation of your story. I will talk more about this in the next chapter.

The way to change what you believe about yourself is to take your faith out of the lies. This is the key to changing your story, this is your dream quest, and nobody can do it but you. It's just you and your story. You have to face your own story, and what you will face, of course, is the main character of your story.

Begin by looking at the main character as if it is somebody else, not you. Your whole life story is like a book about you. Detach from the story and become aware of your own creation. Review the story of your life without any judgment so you won't have any emotional reaction. See your own story since you were a child — all of the growth you have experienced, all of your relationships. Simply take an inventory and perceive the images if you can do that. Imagine that all you have are your lungs to breathe, your eyes to see the beauty, your ears to hear the sounds of nature. It is all about love. Face your life story with your love, and you will experience the most incredible dream quest.

The dream quest is what Buddha did under the bodhi tree, what Jesus did in the desert, and what Moses did on the mountain. All world religions say the same thing because they come from humans who have opened their spiritual eyes and whose faith is no longer blind. But how can they explain the truth to anybody else? Can you imagine Jesus trying to explain the truth two thousand years ago? He talked about truth, forgiveness, and love. He told everybody, "You have to forgive one another. Love is the only way." He gave us the solution for healing the mind, but who was ready back then? Well, the question is: Are we ready now? Do we still want to believe our own lies, and be so blind that we are willing to die for our lies, for our fanaticism, for our dogmas?

Blind faith, as I said before, is leading us to be fanatics, to impose what we believe onto other people without respecting what they believe. We don't need to impose what we believe. We can respect what each of us believes and know that each of us is dreaming our own dream that has nothing to do with anyone else. Just by having this awareness, we are taking a big step toward healing the mind.

The challenge is to recover the power of your faith and no longer be blinded by lies. But if you want to face the tyrant that you have created, you need to have faith. And the problem is that the faith you have invested in your creation is a thousand times stronger than the faith you now have left. So where are you going to find the faith to face your own creation if your creation is eating every ounce of your faith?

Well, if you cannot find faith within you, from what you believe you are, there is a lot of faith outside of you, everywhere. The point is to learn how to gather all of the faith that you need to free yourself from the structure of your lies. That is why humans perform rituals: to gather more faith. When you go to any church and you pray or chant or sing or play the drums or dance, you are gathering power and faith from these rituals. This is really powerful. When you focus your attention on your ritual, this opens a channel to your faith. Your faith follows the ritual, and with your attention hooked into that channel, it is possible to recover your faith.

Ritual can help us to gather faith from nature,

and to build faith with one another as a human community. When people gather together, when they love, they experience tremendous faith. This is what you are doing every time you go to church, any time you pray. When you pray and perform rituals, you gather faith that is not really your own faith, but it is faith that you can use to recover your own. And if you believe 100 percent in what you want to accomplish with a prayer or ritual, you multiply your intent.

When you pray, you commune with the divine spirit. Prayer creates a bridge that goes from the real you into the divine spirit, pushing aside the main character of your story. This is the key, because the main character of your story is the only thing between you and the divine spirit. Prayer and ritual help to stop the judgments and all the voices talking in your head that tell you why something isn't possible. Both prayer and ritual offer an intense action to stop the voice of knowledge from abusing the emotional body.

All the religions with all of their different rituals are wonderful because they provide a way for you to gather the power to break at least some of the self-limiting agreements you have made. Every time you break an agreement, the faith invested in that agreement comes back to you, and you recover a little more of your faith. That is what this book is about. My intent is for you to recover at least part of the faith that you have invested in the main character of your story. But if you gather all of that faith and you don't use it to change the main character of your story, soon all of the faith you have gathered is consumed by the main character.

That is why you need to reclaim your life from the superstition of what you believe you are. There is only one way to do this, and that is to stop believing the storyteller, the voice of knowledge in your head. When you restore your faith in the truth, and you take it out of the lies, the result is that you become authentic. Your emotional body becomes the way it was when you were a child, and you return to your own common sense. I cannot say that I invented this or that I've discovered something new. As an artist, I only rearrange what already exists. Everything I'm sharing with you has been in this world for thousands of years, not only in Mexico, but in Egypt, India, Greece, Rome. Common sense exists in all of us, but we cannot see it with our attention focused on the lies we believe.

Lies make everything complicated, when the truth is very simple. I think now is the time to return to the truth, to common sense, to the simplicity of life itself. Now we know that the lies are so powerful that they blind us. Well, the truth is so powerful that when we finally return to the truth, our entire reality changes. Truth brings us back to paradise, where we experience a strong communion of love with God, with life, with all of creation.

When you release your faith from all the lies, the result is that you free your will. And when your will is free, you can finally make a choice. The voice in your head gives you the illusion that you can make a choice, that you have free will. Well, do you really believe that it's your conscious choice to hurt yourself, to make yourself suffer, to reject and abuse yourself? How can you say that you have free will when you choose to hurt the people you love, when you judge your partner or your children, and make them miserable with your judgment?

Just imagine if you really have free will, which is the power to make your own choices. Do you really choose to sabotage your own happiness or your own love? Do you choose to judge yourself, to blame yourself, to live your life in shame and in guilt? Do you choose to believe that you are bad, that you are not beautiful, that you don't deserve to be happy or healthy or prosperous because you are not worth it? Do you choose to constantly fight with the people you love the most? If you have free will, you choose the opposite. I think it is obvious that our will is *not* free.

When you put your faith in truth instead of in lies, your choices change. When your will is free, your choices come from your integrity, not from the program, that liar in your head. Now you believe whatever you want to believe, and when you have the power to believe whatever you want, something very interesting happens. What you want is to love. You don't want anything else but love because you know that what is not love is not the truth!

When your will is free, you choose happiness and love, peace and harmony. You choose to play; you choose to enjoy life. You no longer choose drama. If in the present moment you are choosing drama, it's because you have no choice; it's a habit. It's because you were programmed to be that way, and you don't even know that you have the power to make a different choice. Something else in your head is making the choice, and it's the voice of the liar. Just like that man in the movie *A Beautiful Mind*, whose visions made the choices for him, your voice is making the choices for you.

Why would we consciously decide to have a fight with our parents or our children or our beloved? It's not that we want to fight. You know, when we are children and we gather with other children, it's because we want to play; we want to have fun and enjoy life. When we grow up and decide to get into a relationship — mainly a romantic relationship — is it because we want to create emotional pain and drama? No, common sense tells us that we want to play together; we want to have fun exploring life together. But the Prince of Lies who controls the voice of knowledge represses our common sense.

Common sense is wisdom, and wisdom is different from knowledge. You are wise when you no longer act against yourself. You are wise when you live in harmony with yourself, with your own kind, with all of creation.

Right now you have a choice. What are you going to do with this information? What happens if you don't believe in lies? Take a moment to put your attention on your feelings, to feel all of the possibilities for your life if your faith is no longer blind. If you recover your faith from lies, your suffering is over, your judgments are over. You no longer live with guilt, with shame, with anger, with jealousy. You no longer have the need to be good enough for anybody, including yourself. You accept what you are, whatever you are, even if you don't know what you are. And you don't care to know anymore. It's not important to know, and that is wisdom.

Just imagine that because you don't believe in lies, your whole life changes. You live your life without trying to control everybody around you, and your integrity doesn't allow anybody to control you. You no longer judge other people or need to complain about whatever they do because you know you can't control what people do. Just imagine that you choose to forgive whoever hurt you in your life because you no longer want to carry all of that emotional poison in your heart. And just by forgiving everybody, even yourself, you heal your mind, you heal your heart, and you no longer have emotional pain.

Just imagine that you recover the power to make your own choices because you no longer believe the storyteller. You enjoy your life with plenitude, with inner peace, with love. Imagine how you treat your partner, how you treat your children, what you teach the new generation, if you no longer believe in lies. Just imagine the change in the whole of humanity out of something so simple: not believing in lies.

✤

POINTS TO PONDER

• The word is pure magic. It is a power that comes directly from God, and faith is the force that directs that power. Everything in our virtual reality is created with the word; we use the word for the creation of our story, to make sense out of everything we experience.

• Faith is the force that gives life to every word, to every belief that we store in our mind. If we agree with a concept, our faith is there, and we keep it in our memory. Faith is the mortar that holds our beliefs together and gives sense and direction to the entire dream.

• The attention is that part of our mind that we use to transfer information from person to person. By hooking the attention, we create a channel of communication, and through that channel we can send and receive information.

• The structure of our knowledge controls the dream of our life because our faith lives in that structure. Our faith is not in the voice of our story, and it's not in our reasoning mind. Our faith is trapped in the structure of our knowledge, and only the truth can set it free.

• Real faith, or free faith, is what you are feeling in this moment. This moment is real; you have faith in life, faith in yourself, faith for no reason. This is the power of your creation in the moment. From this point of power, you can create whatever you want to create in any direction.

• Blind faith leads us nowhere because it doesn't follow the truth. With lies blinding our faith, we fall into the illusion that we are separate from God, and we lose our power of creation.

• When we release our faith from the lies, we recover free will and make our own choices. We recover the power to believe whatever we want to believe. And when we have the power to believe whatever we want, all we want is to love.

9

TRANSFORMING THE STORYTELLER

The Four Agreements as favorite tools

YOU HAVE SEEN HOW YOU CREATE A VIRTUAL REALITY, the dream of your life, and you know that your life is a story. Now with that awareness, the question is: Are you happy with your story? Something important to understand is that you can be whatever you want to be because you are the artist and your life is your creation. It's your story. It's your comedy or your drama, and if the story is changing anyway, then why not direct the change with awareness?

Now that you are an artist with awareness, you can see if you like your art, and you can practice making it better. Practice makes the master. But it's action that makes the difference. When I discovered this, my action was to take responsibility for my art and purify my program. As an artist I started exploring the possibilities — every action and every reaction. And by the way, this is our real nature: to explore. Explore what? Life! What else can we explore?

To change the story of your life is what the Toltec call *the mastery of transformation*. It's about transforming you, the storyteller, the dreamer. Life is changing so fast, and you can see that you are always transforming, but you master transformation when you no longer resist change. Instead, you take advantage of change, and you enjoy change. To master transformation is to live in the present moment, all the time. Life is an eternal *now* because the force of life is creating everything right now, and it is transforming everything right now.

How are you going to change your story? Well, now you know that you are creating your story according to what you believe about yourself. The way to transform what you believe about yourself is to unlearn what you have already learned. When you unlearn, your faith returns to you, your personal power increases, and you can invest your faith in new beliefs.

If you want to know the truth, if you are ready to take your faith out of the lies, then remember: *Don't believe yourself,* and *don't believe anybody else.* This will give you clarity about many things. But you may need a little support to stop believing the lies, and to start breaking all of the agreements that go against yourself. The Four Agreements offer this support. They are just for you, the main character of your story. These four simple agreements can take you all the way to your integrity: *Be impeccable with your word. Don't take anything personally. Don't make assumptions. Always do your best.*

Many tools can help you change your story, but the Four Agreements are my favorite tools for transformation. Why? Because they have the power to help you unlearn the many ways you have learned to use the word against yourself. Just by following these agreements, you challenge all of the opinions that are nothing but superstition and lies. *Be impeccable with your word* because you use the word to create your story. *Don't take anything personally* because you live in your own story and other people live in their own story. *Don't make assumptions* because most assumptions are not the truth; they are fiction, and when the storyteller makes up stories — especially about other storytellers — this creates big drama. *Always do your best* because this keeps the voice of knowledge from judging you, and by taking action, you keep the voice from talking to you.

The storyteller, the liar in your head, makes you use your word against yourself. It makes you take everything personally, it makes a lot of assumptions, and it makes you fail to do your best. The first agreement, *be impeccable with your word*, is the supreme agreement because it helps you to recognize all of the lies that rule your life. To be impeccable is to use the power of your word in the direction of truth and love. The other three agreements are more support for the first agreement — they are the practice that makes the master — but the goal is the first agreement. By practicing all Four Agreements, the moment comes when you experience the truth and your emotional reaction is incredible.

I have written a book about the Four Agreements, and I tried to keep it as simple as possible. The book can make you feel as if you already know the Four Agreements. And this is true because the agreements come from the real you, and the real you is exactly the real me, too. Your spirit is telling you the same thing, and it's pure common sense. The book is a messenger of love. It is like an open doorway that will take you all the way to the real you, but you are the one who needs to walk the way. You need to have the courage to apply the tools to find yourself, and to recreate your own story in your own way. You can transform your entire story just by practicing the Four Agreements. Let's take a closer look at each agreement.

The first agreement, *be impeccable with your word,* means you never use the power of the word against yourself in the creation of your story. *Impeccable* means "without sin." Anything you do that goes against yourself is a sin. When you believe in lies, you are using the power of the word against yourself. When you believe that nobody likes you, that nobody understands you, that you will never make it, you are using the word against yourself.

Many philosophies around the world have known that lies are a distortion of the word, and some traditions call this distortion *evil.* I prefer to say that we are *using the word against ourselves* because we do not call it *evil* when we judge ourselves and find ourselves guilty. We do not call it *evil* when we reject ourselves and treat ourselves much worse than the way we treat our pets. When you are impeccable, you never speak against yourself, you have no beliefs that go against yourself, and you never help anybody else to go against you. To be impeccable means that you don't use your own knowledge against yourself, and you don't allow the voice in your head to abuse you. Maybe the first agreement, *be impeccable with your word*, makes a little more sense now.

Remember, the word is your power because you use the word for the creation of your virtual world. You use the word to create the main character of your story. Every self-opinion, every belief, is made by words: "I am smart, I am stupid, I am beautiful, I am ugly." This is powerful. But your word is even more powerful because it also represents you when you interact with other dreamers. Every time you speak, your thought becomes sound, your thought becomes the word, and now it can go into other people's minds. If their minds are fertile for that kind of seed, they eat it, and now that thought lives inside of them, too.

The word is a force that you cannot see, but you can see the manifestation of the force, the expression of the word, which is your own life. The way to measure how you use the word is by your emotional reaction. How do you know when you are using the word impeccably? Well, you are happy. You feel good about yourself. You feel love. How do you know when you are using the word against yourself? Well, when you are suffering with envy, with anger, with sadness. Suffering of all kinds is the result of misusing the word; it is the result of believing in knowledge contaminated with lies. If you clean up the word, you recover the impeccability of the word, and you never betray yourself. If you agree to be impeccable with your word, this is enough for you to return to the paradise that humans lost. It is enough to bring you back to the truth and to transform your whole story. Be impeccable with your word. Very simple.

The second agreement, *don't take anything personally*, helps you to break the many lies you agreed to believe in. When you take things personally, you react and feel hurt, and this creates emotional poison. Then you want revenge, you want to get even, and you use the word against other people. Now you know that whatever somebody projects onto you is just like Picasso saying, "This is you." You know that it's just the person's storyteller, simply telling you a story. Not taking anything personally gives you immunity to emotional poison in all your relationships. You no longer lose control and react because you are emotionally hurt. This gives you clarity, which puts you a step ahead of other people who cannot see their own stories.

The second agreement guides you in breaking hundreds of little lies until it hits the core of all of the lies in your life. When this happens, the whole edifice of knowledge collapses, and you have a second chance to create another story, in your own way. The Toltec call this *losing the human form.*

When you lose the human form, you have the opportunity to choose what to believe according to your integrity. When you were a child, you used your attention to create the first dream of your life. You never had the opportunity to make a choice about what to believe; everything you agreed to believe was imposed upon you. Now you have an opportunity you didn't have when you were a child. You can use your attention for the second time to base your story on the truth instead of on lies. The Toltec call this *the dream of the second attention*. I call it *your second story* because it's still a dream, it's still a story! But now it's your choice.

When you lose the human form, your will is free again. You recover the power of your faith, and what you can do with that faith has no limits. You can recreate your life in a big way if this is what you want. But the goal is not to save the world. No, the only mission that you have in life is to make yourself happy. That's it. It's that simple. And the only way that you can make yourself happy is to create a story that will make you happy. Anything can happen to any of us. You cannot control what is happening around you, but you can control the way you tell the story. You can relate the story as a big melodrama and be sad and depressed about everything that happens to you, or you can relate the story without all of the drama.

The third agreement, *don't make assumptions*, is a big ticket to personal freedom. What is going on when we make assumptions? The storyteller is making up a story, we believe the story, and we fail to ask questions that might shed some light on the truth. Most of our dream is based on assumptions, and these assumptions create a whole world of illusion that is not true at all, but we believe it. Making assumptions and then taking them personally is the beginning of hell in this world. Humans create so many problems because we make assumptions and believe they are the truth! Almost all of our conflicts are based on this.

To be aware is to see what is truth, to see everything the way it is, not the way we want it to be to justify what we already believe. The *mastery of awareness* is the first mastery of the Toltec, and we can also call it the *mastery of truth*. First, you need to be aware that the voice in your head is always telling you a story. You are dreaming all the time. It is true that you perceive, but the way the storyteller justifies, explains, and makes assumptions about what you perceive is not the truth; it's just a story.

Next, you need to have the awareness that the voice of the storyteller in your head is not necessarily your voice. Every concept in your head has a voice that wants to express itself. It is dreaming. It is just a story trying to catch your attention and justify its own existence. The other part of you, the part who is listening, the one who is dreaming the dream, is the one who is being abused.

Finally, you need to practice awareness until you master awareness. When you master awareness as a habit, you always see life the way it is, not the way you want to see it. You no longer try to put things into words, to explain anything to yourself, and this keeps you from making assumptions. You only use the word to communicate with others, knowing that what you are communicating is just a point of view based on what you believe. And what you believe is just a program; it is nothing but ideas that are mostly lies. That is why you need to listen and ask questions. With clear communication, people will give you all of the information you need, and you won't have to make assumptions.

The fourth agreement is *always do your best*. When you do your best, you don't give the voice of knowledge an opportunity to judge you. If the voice doesn't judge you, there's no need to feel guilty or to punish yourself. Doing your best, you are going to be productive, which means you are going to take action. Doing your best is about taking action and doing what you love to do because it's the action that makes you happy. You are doing it because you want to, not because you have to.

The best moments of your life are when you are authentic, when you are being yourself. When you are in your creation and you are doing what you love to do, you become what you really are again. You are not thinking in that moment; you are expressing. When you are doing your best in your creation, the mind stops. You are alive again. Your emotions are coming out and you don't even notice how great you feel. The action, just the action, makes you feel great. When you have inaction, your mind has to have action, and that is an open invitation for the voice of knowledge to talk to you. But when you are absorbed in what you are doing, the mind hardly speaks.

When you are creating, the voice of knowledge is not there, even if you are using words in your art. If you are writing a poem, you are not thinking about the words you will use to write the poem; you are simply expressing your emotions. The words are the instrument; they are the code that you use for expression. If you are a musician who is playing music, there is no difference between you and the music. At the same time you are creating the music, you are the one who is enjoying every note, every sound. You become one with what you are doing, and it's a supreme pleasure. Anyone who is a musician will know what I am talking about. You are expressing what you really are, and this is the greatest thing that can happen to anybody. Just expressing yourself leads you into ecstasy because you are creating. This is life as an art.

Doing your best is about trusting in yourself and trusting in creation, the force of life. You set a goal and go for it 100 percent without any attachment to attaining it. You don't know if you are going to reach your goal, and you don't care if you do. You go for it, and when you reach the goal it's wonderful. And if you don't reach the goal, that's wonderful, too. Either way, you are complete because love in motion is a wonderful thing. Taking action is an expression of yourself, it's the expression of the spirit, and it's your creation.

I encourage you to take responsibility for every decision you make in life. No decision is right or wrong; what matters is the action that follows your

choice. Everything in life is just a choice. You control the dream by making choices. Every choice has
a consequence, and a dream master is aware of the
consequences. We can also say that for every action,
we experience a reaction. If your knowledge is the
action, and your emotions are the reaction, then you
can see why becoming aware of the voice of knowledge is so important.

The voice of knowledge is always sabotaging
your happiness. In the happiest moments of your
life, you are playing; you are acting like a child. But
the voice comes into your head and says, "This is
too good to be true. Let's put our feet back on the
ground and get back to reality." And the reality that
the voice of knowledge is talking about is suffering.

Life can be so wonderful. If you love yourself,
if you practice doing your best, very soon it becomes
a habit. When doing your best becomes a habit,
everything is a set up for you to always be happy,
just as you were when you were a very young child.
But first you need to stop the internal dialogue. This

is one of the biggest miracles that any human can experience. If you can stop the voice from talking to you, then you are almost free from being abused by all of the lies.

People have asked me if I encourage the use of a mantra to eliminate the internal dialogue. Well, I encourage you to use any trick that you can find to stop the chatter. There is no kitchen recipe. You can explore any number of ways until you find your own way. For some people, a mantra might be the miracle. For other people, meditation, contemplation, or music could be the miracle. For others, walking outdoors or just surrounding themselves with natural beauty could be the miracle. It could be dancing, yoga, running, swimming, or any exercise. It's up to you.

When I was a teenager, my grandfather told me, "Music is the solution to stopping the voice in your head. Replace the voice with music, because you cannot explain music. How can you explain the Fifth Symphony of Beethoven? You can use your opinions, but you can't explain it. You need to play it."

I understood what my grandfather said, but I didn't like his music. My grandfather liked classical music, so I refused that method completely. I told him, "I don't think so. It's boring." Of course, I was listening to music anyway, but the music I liked was the Beatles. Well, the lyrics were in English, and I only spoke Spanish at the time. I knew every word to the songs, but the words had no meaning for me. If there was any drama in those songs, I didn't perceive it as drama; I perceived it as beauty.

Listening to the Beatles really worked for me because the voices were just like another instrument, and the music occupied the space of the voice of knowledge. There were times when the voice was there, but there were times when there was no voice. I liked the music so much that if I was not putting my attention on anything else, there was only music in my head. I started doing this without awareness because although I had heard what my grandfather said, I had made the assumption that he was talking about classical music! Well, the music can be drums, trumpets, or any kind of instrument as long as there are no words in a language that you know to hook your attention. The problem is when the music has words that have meaning to you, and you can think about the words.

There are many ways to quiet the mind if you just use them, but from my point of view, practicing the Four Agreements is the best way. These agreements have the power to break thousands of little agreements that go against yourself, but they are not as simple as they look. Many people say, "I understand the Four Agreements, and they are changing my life, but at a certain point I cannot keep going." Well, you cannot keep going because in that moment you are facing a strong belief. And the faith you invested in that belief is stronger than the faith you have available to change that belief. That is why it's important to practice recovering your faith with little beliefs. Then you can go for the stronger beliefs.

Every time you practice the Four Agreements, their meaning goes a little deeper. When you read the book *The Four Agreements* for the second time, or the third time, at a certain point it seems as if you are reading a different book. And it seems like a different book because you have already broken many little agreements. Now you can go a little deeper, and you go deeper and deeper until the moment comes when you open your spiritual eyes. When you finally transform, your life becomes a masterpiece of dreaming, an expression of your emotional body, just the way it was before knowledge.

❧

POINTS TO PONDER

• The way to transform what you believe about yourself is to unlearn what you have already learned. When you unlearn, your faith returns to you, your personal power increases, and you can invest your faith in new beliefs.

• The Four Agreements have the power to help you unlearn the many ways you have learned to use the word against yourself. By following these agreements, you challenge all of the opinions that are nothing but superstition and lies: *Be impeccable with your word. Don't take anything personally. Don't make assumptions. Always do your best.*

• When the edifice of knowledge collapses, you have a second chance to create a story according to your integrity. You can use your attention for the second time to make a story based on the truth instead of on lies. In *the dream of the second attention*, you recover the power of your faith, your will is free again, and what you can do with that has no limits.

• When you are absorbed in what you are doing, the mind hardly speaks. You are expressing what you really are, and just the action makes it great. When there is inaction, your mind has to have action, and that is an open invitation for the voice of knowledge to talk to you.

• The best moments of your life are when you are authentic, when you are being yourself. When you are in your creation and you are doing what you love to do, you become what you really are again. You are not thinking in that moment; you are expressing. Your emotions are coming out and you feel great.

• Every time you practice the Four Agreements, their meaning goes deeper and deeper until the moment comes when you open your spiritual eyes. Then your life becomes an expression of your emotional body, just the way it was before knowledge.

10

Writing Our Story with Love

Life as an ongoing romance

What is the best way to write your life story? There is only one way, and that way is with love. Love is the material I use to write my story because love comes directly from my integrity, from what I really am. I love the main character of my story, and the main character loves and enjoys every secondary character. I am not afraid to tell you, "I love you."

Your mind may say, "How can you love me when you don't even know me?" I don't need to know you. I don't need to justify my love. I love you because this is my pleasure. Love coming out of me makes me happy, and it's not important if you reject me because I don't reject myself. In my story, I live in an ongoing romance, and everything is beautiful for me.

To live in love is to be alive again. It is to return to your integrity, to what you were before knowledge. When you recover your integrity, you always follow love. You live your life as an eternal romance because when you love yourself, it is easy to love everybody else. You feel so good just being by yourself, and when you gather with other people, it's because you want to share your happiness. You love so much that you don't need anybody's love to make you happy. But this doesn't mean that you don't accept love. Of course you accept love. You accept good food, good wine, good music, why not good love?

If you can see yourself as an artist, and you can

see that your life is your own creation, then why not create the most beautiful story for yourself? It's your story, and it's just a choice. You can write a story based on love and romance, but that love has to begin with yourself. I suggest that you start a brand-new relationship between you and yourself. You can have the most wonderful, romantic love relationship, and the way to have it is by changing your agreements.

One agreement you can make is to treat yourself with respect. Introduce the agreement of self-respect, and tell the voice in your head, "It's time for us to respect each other." Many of the judgments will end there, and most of the self-rejection will end there, too. Then you can allow the voice to talk, but the dialogue will be much better. You will have all of these great ideas, these great dialogues in your head, and when you express them to other people, they will love what you are saying. You will find yourself smiling and having fun, even when you are just by yourself.

You can see why the relationship with yourself is so important. When you have conflict with yourself, when you don't like yourself, or even worse, when you hate yourself, the internal dialogue is contaminated with poison, and that is the way you talk to yourself. When you love yourself, even if the voice of knowledge is in your head, it is nice to you. When you love yourself, when you are kind to yourself, that is a good relationship with yourself. Then every relationship you have will improve, but it always begins with yourself.

How can we expect to be kind when we speak with other people if we are not kind to ourselves? We have the need to express what we feel, and we express our emotions through our voice. If we don't feel good, if we are full of emotional poison, we need to release it. That is why we have the need to curse, to release all of the emotions that are trapped in our head. If we have anger or jealousy that needs to come out, our words will carry those emotions. If the voice of knowledge is abusing us, then that voice will treat others the same way. If we are having fun with our-selves, that is what we project to the outside.

The first step toward improving your relation-ship with yourself is to accept yourself just the way you are. You don't need to learn *how* to love your-self. You need to unlearn all of the reasons why you reject yourself, and by nature you love yourself. You love not the *image* you project or the *way* you are, but you love yourself because of *what* you are. Then you start to enjoy yourself until you love yourself so much that you give yourself everything you need. You don't leave yourself until last anymore. The more you enjoy the presence of yourself, the more you enjoy your life, and the more you enjoy the presence of everyone around you.

When you love, you honor and respect *life*. When you live your life with love, honor, and respect, the story you create is an ongoing romance. To love life is to enjoy every manifestation of life, and it is effortless. It is as easy as inhaling and exhaling. To breathe is the greatest need of the human body, and air is the greatest gift. You can be so grateful for the air that just to breathe is enough to love. How can you show your gratitude for the gift of air? By enjoying every breath. When you focus on that enjoyment, you can make it a habit to enjoy the air, and you can enjoy it at least seventeen or eighteen times per minute. Just to breathe is enough to always be happy, to always be in love.

But this is just one direction that love can take. Every activity of our life can become a ritual of love. We have the need for food, and we can do the same thing with food that we do with air. Food is also love, and when we enjoy our food, when we really taste it and feel the texture, it is one of the most sensual experiences we can have. There is so much love in the action of eating, and if we use a new mantra every time we eat, we increase the pleasure. The mantra is just one sound: "Mmmm." If we practice loving our food every time we eat, soon it becomes a habit. It becomes a ritual that we use to give our thanks, to express our love, and to receive love without resistance.

Communication can be another way to express

our love. Every time we share our story or listen to another person's story, we can practice sharing our love. One of the assignments I used to give my apprentices was to find at least a thousand different ways of saying "I love you" in one week. When you practice all of these different ways of saying "I love you," your heart opens completely to hear the whole of creation telling you, "I love you." And you don't need to justify or explain that love. You just receive love and give love without even trying to understand or make a story about it.

When you have the courage to open your heart completely to love, a miracle happens. You start perceiving the reflection of your love in everything. Then eating, walking, talking, singing, dancing, showering, working, playing — everything you do becomes a ritual of love. When everything becomes a ritual of love, you are no longer thinking; you are feeling and enjoying life. You find pleasure in every activity you do because you love to do it. Just to be alive is wonderful, and you feel intensely happy.

People have asked me, "Miguel, are you happy all the time? Don't you ever get cranky?" Well, to be cranky is completely normal. Sometimes I'm cranky when I don't get enough sleep. If I only sleep two hours in the night, I don't feel good when I awaken; I feel *rrrraar!* But that *rrraar* is not directed toward anybody. Why should I be unkind to anybody just because I'm feeling bad and my body is telling me I want to sleep more? If in that moment I cannot satisfy my body, I finish doing whatever I have to do, and then I take my body to a bed and put my body to sleep.

I have the right to feel cranky, but that doesn't mean I'm going to hurt my beloved or my children or my friends or the people who work for me. If we are selfish and we feel cranky, then we believe that nobody has the right to be happy around us. Then we say, "Why are you laughing when I feel so bad?" This is nothing but selfishness, and we are selfish with others because we are selfish with ourselves. Whatever we feel for ourselves, we project onto others. The way we treat ourselves is the way we treat others.

Writing your story with love is so easy to do. Why make it complicated and difficult when love is your true nature? By not being what you are, you resist love, and you are afraid to love because you believe one of the biggest lies, and that lie is "love hurts." As I said before, love doesn't hurt. Love gives us pleasure. But you can even use love to hurt yourself. Someone may really love you, but you don't appreciate that love because you are hearing your own lies. You can say, "What does that person want from me? He wants to take advantage of me." Who knows what the storyteller will tell you?

If you don't perceive love, if you cannot recognize love, it's because you only recognize the poison inside you. I am responsible for what I say, but I am not responsible for what you understand. I can give you my love, but you can make the interpretation that you are receiving judgments, or who knows? Only your storyteller knows. When we no longer believe our own stories, we find it so easy to enjoy one another.

Humans are made for love. Before knowledge, it was easy to open our heart and to love, and we just walked away from whatever was not love. But with the voice of knowledge in our head, we walk away from love, and we go for what is not love. We always have a choice, and if we love ourselves, we choose love. We do not allow ourselves to be hurt by accepting other people's opinions or abuse. If other people abuse us, they are abusing us because we stay there, because we allow that to happen. And if we stay, it's because we believe that we deserve the abuse, and we are using them for self-punishment. If we don't have awareness, we blame, when the solution is not to blame. The solution is to step aside and not be there.

How can you believe someone who says, "I love you," and then treats you with disrespect and emotional violence? How can someone say, "I love you," when that person wants to control your life, to tell you what you have to do, what you have to believe? How can someone claim to love you, and then give you emotional garbage, jealousy, and envy?

How can we tell someone, "I love you," and then send all our opinions against the person we love and try to make that person suffer? I have to tell you what is wrong with you because "I love you." I have to judge you, find you guilty, and punish you because "I love you." I have to make you wrong all the time, and make you feel like you are good for nothing because "I love you." And because you love me, you have to put up with my anger, with my jealousy, with all my stupidity.

Do you think this is love? This is not love. This is nothing but selfishness, and we call it love. And we say "love hurts," but we are hurting ourselves with our own lies. All of the struggle in romantic relationships is just nonsense. It is not love, and that is why people are starving for love.

When you are needy, this is what you share in a relationship. But when you are open to love, you receive love, and if it's not love, you don't have to be there. You are open to receiving love, but you are not open to receiving abuse. You are not open to being blamed; you are not open to receiving anybody's poison because your mind is no longer fertile ground for that. When you love and respect yourself, there is no way that you ever allow anybody to disrespect you or dishonor you.

Many people come to me and say, "Gosh, I want someone who loves me. I want the right man or the right woman to come into my life." Who is the right man or the right woman? It's not about them; it's about you. If that person comes into your life, and you treat that person the way you treat yourself, which means with selfishness, then you are going to use that person to hurt yourself.

How can we want a romantic relationship when we don't even like ourselves? How can we pretend to love somebody else when we don't love ourselves? When you feel unworthy, when you don't respect yourself, you don't respect your partner either. If you don't honor yourself, how can you honor your partner? How can you give anything that you don't have for yourself?

The most beautiful and romantic relationship has to begin with you. You are responsible for one half of the relationship: your half. When you respect yourself, you respect your beloved. When you honor yourself, you honor your beloved. And you give love and accept love. But when you are full of poison, this is what you give. When you abuse yourself, you want to abuse your beloved. It's just nonsense.

When you hear people's stories, including your own, you hear nothing but lies. But behind the story, everything is love, which means everything and everybody is divine. You are divine, you are perfect, but as an artist, you create your own story and you have the illusion that the story is real. You live your life by justifying that story. And by justifying the story, you are wasting your life.

As I've said before, life is very short. You don't know if your children, or your friends, or your beloved will still be here tomorrow. Just imagine that your opinion is so important that you have a big fight with your partner or your child. You lose control because of all of the lies you believe, and you really hurt your loved one. The next day you discover that your loved one is dead. How will you feel about telling your loved one all of those things you didn't really mean?

Our life is so short that every time I see my children, I enjoy them as much as I can. Whenever I can, I enjoy my beloved, my family, my friends, my apprentices. But mainly I enjoy myself, because I am with myself all the time. Why should I spend my precious time with myself judging myself, rejecting myself, creating guilt and shame? Why should I push myself to be angry or jealous? If I don't feel good emotionally, I find out what is causing it and I fix it. Then I can recover my happiness and keep going with my story.

When you write your story with love, you love the main character unconditionally. That is the biggest difference between the old story based on lies and the new story based on love. When you love yourself unconditionally, you justify and explain everything you perceive through the eyes of love. When that new main character hooks your attention, your attention is focused on love. Now it is easy to love all the secondary characters of the story unconditionally because that is the nature of the new main character. This is wisdom; it is simple common sense, and it's the goal of all the different traditions and religions around the world.

Love is so simple, so easy and wonderful, but love begins with you. Every relationship improves when you love yourself and live with awareness of your love. Few people know how to love with awareness, but everybody knows how to love without awareness. When you love without awareness, you don't even notice that it's love you're feeling. You see a little child smiling at you, and you feel something for that child. This is love, but of course the voice of knowledge tells you, "This is not love."

You love so many times, and you don't even notice that you love.

Love and respect are what we should also teach our children, but the only way to teach them love and respect is to love and respect ourselves. There is no other way. Again, we can only give what we have, not what we don't have. I can only share what I know. I cannot tell you anything that I don't know. My parents taught me what they learned from their parents. How could they teach me something different? They could not do better than that. I cannot blame my parents for the programming I received. I cannot blame my teachers for the training I received in school. They did their best; it was the only thing they knew, and they passed it on to the next generation.

The only chance to break the chain of lies is to change the adults, to change ourselves. Children are very aware. They learn from what we do; they learn what they see, not just what we say. We tell them, "Never lie to anybody." Later, somebody is knocking on the door, and we say, "Tell them I'm not here."

Whatever we do at home, the way we behave, the way we treat one another, is what our children learn. If we are never at home, that becomes normal behavior for them. When they grow up, they are not at home either, and their children are alone. The way we speak is the way they speak. If we curse at home, they curse, too. If they receive violence, they deliver violence. If we fight and share our anger and our poison, our children learn that this is the normal way of being, and this is how they learn to write their own stories. But if there is respect and honor at home, if there is love at home, this is what they learn.

By changing ourselves, by loving ourselves, the message we deliver to our children carries the seeds of love and truth. These seeds go into our children, and these seeds can change their lives. Imagine how our children will grow up when we share with them the seeds of love instead of the seeds of fear, judgment, shame, or blame. Imagine how they will grow up when we finally respect them as humans just like us, and we don't try to break their integrity because we are bigger and stronger. Imagine when we teach our children to be secure in themselves, and to have their own voice. Imagine how everything will change if we bring respect to any relationship.

People have asked me why I don't work with children, and the reason is because they have parents. It doesn't matter what I tell children; it is undone by their parents. I prefer to teach parents and teachers because our children learn from them. Our future as a human race depends on children. Children will take our place one day, and we are training them to be like us. Just imagine if your parents had told you a different story when you were a child. Your life story would be completely different. But you can still change your story, and if you have children, the only way to change their story is to change your own.

To love is so easy; it's not work at all. But we have so much work to do, and that work is to unlearn all of the lies that we believe. Unlearning lies is not easy because we feel safe with our lies; we are very attached to them. But the more we practice seeing the truth, the easier it becomes to detach from our lies. Transforming our life gets easier with practice, and our life gets better and better.

The more love we have, the more love we can share and receive. To give to one another and receive from one another is the purpose of a relationship. We don't need a lot of words. When we share time with someone, what is important is to communicate with feelings, not with words. But if we want to share words, we don't need anything complicated. It's just three words: "I love you." That's it. What makes you happy is not the love that other people feel for you, but the love you feel for other people.

Once we experience love, we can't find the words to explain what we really feel, but to love is the greatest experience that any of us can have. To experience love is to experience God; it is to experience heaven right here and now. When the voice of knowledge is no longer hooking our attention, our perception becomes much wider. We start perceiving our own emotional reactions, and we start perceiving other people's emotional reactions. Then we start perceiving the emotions that come from the trees, from the flowers, from the clouds, from everything. We see love coming from everywhere, even from other people. At a certain point, we are simply in ecstasy, and there are no words to explain it because there are no agreements yet about how to explain it.

What we call *love* is something that is so generic that it's not even what love really is. Love is much more than words can describe. As I said before, we cannot really talk about the truth; we need to experience the truth. The same is true of love. The only way to really know love is to experience love, to have the courage to jump into the ocean of love, and perceive it in its totality. That is the only way, but we are programmed with so much fear that we don't see the love coming from all around us. We look for love in other people when they don't love themselves. Of course we won't find love there; we only find selfishness and a war of control.

You don't have to search for love. Love is here because God is here; the force of *life* is everywhere. We humans create the story of separation, and we search for what we believe we don't have. We search for perfection, for love, for truth, for justice, and we search and search when everything is inside of us. Everything is here; we just need to open our spiritual eyes to see it.

There is nothing you need to do to improve what you really are. The only thing left for all of us to do is to create a beautiful story and enjoy a better life. How do you create a beautiful story? By being authentic. When the main character is authentic, it is easy to write your story with integrity, with common sense, with love.

Life is the greatest gift that we receive, and the art of living is the greatest art. How do you master the art of living? Practice makes the master. It's not about learning; it's about taking action and practicing your art. As an artist, if you practice love, and you keep practicing and practicing, the moment comes when everything you do is an expression of your love. How will you know when you have mastered love? When the story you tell yourself is an ongoing romance.

※

POINTS TO PONDER

• The best way to write your story is with love. Love is the material that comes directly from your integrity, from what you really are.

• When you introduce the agreement of self-respect, many self-judgments end there, and most of the self-rejection ends there, too. Then you can allow the voice to talk, but the dialogue is much better. You find yourself smiling and having fun, even when you are just by yourself.

• When you enjoy the presence of yourself, you love yourself not because of the way you are, but because of *what* you are. The more you love yourself, the more you enjoy your life, and the more you enjoy the presence of everyone around you.

• Every activity of your life can become a ritual of love — eating, walking, talking, working, playing. When everything becomes a ritual of love, you are no longer thinking; you are feeling. Just to be alive makes you intensely happy.

• When you love yourself unconditionally, you justify and explain everything you perceive through the eyes of love. Your attention is focused on love, and this makes it easy to feel unconditional love for all of the secondary characters in your story.

• The only way to know love is to experience love, to have the courage to jump into the ocean of love, and perceive it in its totality. Once you experience love, you can't find the words to explain what you feel, but you see love coming from everyone, from everything, from everywhere.

11

OPENING OUR SPIRITUAL EYES

A reality of love all around us

ANOTHER OPPORTUNITY FOR ME TO ENCOUNTER the truth occurred during a car accident that was so dramatic that I almost died. There are no words to explain what I experienced, but the truth made it obvious that what I believed was a lie. Like most people, I used to believe that I am my mind and I am my physical body. I live in my physical body; it is home, and I can touch it. Then, in my near-death experience, I could see my physical body asleep at the wheel of my car. If I was perceiving my physical body from outside my body, then it was obvious that I am not my mind, and I am not my physical body. Then the question became: *What am I?*

In the moment when I came face to face with death, I started to perceive another reality. My attention expanded so much that there was no future or past; there was only the eternal now. Light was everywhere, and everything was full of light. I could feel my perception go through all of these different realities until I recovered the attention and could focus on one universe at a time. I was in the light, and it was a moment of total awareness, of pure perception. At a certain point, I knew that the light has all the information about everything and that everything is alive. I can say that I was with God, that I was in bliss, that I was in a state of ecstasy, but these are just words that I know.

After the accident, my perception of the world

changed again because I knew, not just as a theory, that I am not this physical body. And I began a search that was different from my search before the accident. Before the accident, I was still searching for perfection, for an image to satisfy the main character of my story. After the accident, I knew that what I was searching for was something I had lost: myself.

It took more than a year for me to recover from the impact of seeing my own creation from outside my body. My first reaction after the accident was to try to deny what had happened. I tried to feel safe in my world of lies and tell myself, "This is not true; it is just an illusion." I thought that surely it was just a hallucination caused by the accident. I created all kinds of stories to justify that experience, and I know that many people do the same thing. They try to forget about it, to keep going with their ordinary story. But something deep inside was telling me, "No, this is real." Fortunately for me, I felt the doubt and thought, "What if that experience was real and everything else in my life was the illusion?"

After that experience, I wasn't the same because I couldn't believe my own story anymore. I needed many answers, and I started to read every kind of book to try to find them. Some people described a similar experience, but hardly anybody could explain what happened. I finished medical school, returned to my home, and went directly to my grandfather to tell him about my experience. He just laughed and said, "I knew that life would have to make you see the truth the hard way. And that is what happened to you because you have always been very stubborn."

I told my grandfather that I wanted to experience that reality again to see if it was true — without an accident, of course. My grandfather told me, "Well, the only way you can do it is to let go of everything, just the way you did in the moment when you died. When you die, you lose everything, and if you live your life as if you've already lost everything, you will have the experience again." He gave me many clues, and I tried many times to do what he told me, but I failed. My grandfather died, and I hadn't made it yet.

The next in line was my mother, and her explanation was a little different. She told me, "The only way for you to experience that reality is to master *dreaming*. To do this, you have to completely detach from what you believe you are; you have to let go of the story of your life. It's just like the moment right before your brain goes to sleep — when you are so tired that you cannot keep your eyes open any longer. In that moment, you detach from everything; you don't care about anything in your story because you just want to sleep. When you can do this without falling asleep, you will have the experience again."

I asked my mother to help me, and because she felt compassion for me, she chose twenty-one people to train in dreaming. Every Sunday for three years, we went into dreaming for eight to twelve hours. Not one of the twenty-one people ever missed a Sunday. There were eight or nine medical doctors, lawyers, and a variety of people with a lot of personal importance in the group. But according to my mother, only three of us really made it. Fortunately, I was one of them, and after the first year of dreaming, I finally had the experience again with full awareness. That was it; after that point, the other two years of dreaming were the greatest experience of my life.

Each time I went into the state of ecstasy, I was able to stay there a little longer. Then, a few days later, I would lose it again and be back to the way I had been almost all of my life. Errrh! I was determined to experience that state all the time. There was no way I could live my life any differently. It took me three or four months to have the experience for the third time, but it happened again, and now I was staying longer. It became easier and easier, and every time I stayed longer and longer until that state became my normal reality.

At first it was difficult to function in ordinary reality, especially in a hospital as a medical doctor.

I felt like nothing made sense to me, but in some ways, I was functioning better. It was as though I could see two realities at the same time. I could see what really is, but I could also see the stories. And it was a big shock at a certain point just to see myself lying, and to see everybody around me lying. Though I didn't have any judgment about it, I could see that people were making nonsense of their life. I could see them creating drama and emotional pain. They would get so upset over something that wasn't important. They would make up stories and lie about everything. It was amazing and even kind of funny to watch them do it. But I had to refrain from laughing because I knew they would take it personally. They could not see their own stories because they were blind.

People have the right to live their life in any way they want to live it. But if you have had the experience I've been describing, you understand. Certainly many people have had the same experience, but then fear makes them try to deny what happened. Many times when I've given workshops, I see people go so high into love, and they understand a great deal. But if they see something in their story that they don't like, they just deny the whole experience and run away. And if the truth hits their personal importance, they devalue everything, and run away with a lot of judgments. I see this happen all the time, but it's okay because that is all the truth they can handle.

It took many years for me to win the conflict between the truth and what is not the truth because our lies are so seductive. The temptation to believe in lies is very strong, but the car accident pushed me to another point of reference. And, yes, now I know that there is another reality right here and right now, and it is more than the reality of light and sound that we normally perceive. There are many realities that exist, but we only perceive the reality where we focus our attention.

I can say according to my story that the reality I experienced is a reality of love. The energy of love is just like the light that comes from the sun. The sunlight splits into thousands of different colors, and the light looks different depending on what is reflecting the light. That is why we can see different colors, different shapes, and different forms. Well, for me, the same thing happens in this reality of love. You perceive the reflection of the emotions coming from every object, and as with light, the emotion of love looks different depending on what is reflecting the love. The emotional body creates an entire reality right in front of your eyes, in the same place that the reality of light exists. Of course, it's almost impossible to put it into words, but I think it's worth trying.

I want you to use your imagination to try to understand what I am saying. I want you to imagine that humans have been blind for thousands of years. We have no idea that light exists because we just don't open our eyes. But we develop the rest of our senses, and we create an entire virtual reality through sound. Like bats, we recognize objects through the reflection of sound. We give names to every object and emotion; we create a language, we create knowl-edge, and we communicate through sound. That is our reality — a reality of sound.

Then imagine that for the first time in your life, you open your eyes and you perceive light. Suddenly a reality full of objects, shapes, and colors appears in front of you. You cannot comprehend this reality because you have never seen light before. For the first time, you see flowers and clouds and grass and but-terflies. You see the rain, the snow, the oceans, the stars, the moon, the sun. Perhaps you don't even per-ceive these things as separate objects because you have no idea what you are perceiving. You cannot name anything you see; there are no words to describe your experience. You have to use the universe of sound to explain the universe of light. You try to compare colors with sounds, shapes with melodies. You say, "The color red is like this kind of tone in the musi-cal scale. The ocean is like this symphony."

Imagine your emotional reaction to seeing so much color and beauty for the first time. You are

overwhelmed with emotion, and tears flow out of
your eyes. Just by perceiving all of this beauty, your
heart begins to open wide and love starts pouring
out of you. If you try to describe your emotions, you
say, "I'm in bliss. I'm in ecstasy. I'm in a state of
grace." Then you close your eyes, and again you perceive only the reality of sound. Now even if you
want to, you cannot open your eyes again.

How can you explain that experience to yourself
when there are no words to explain it? How can you
explain a color or a shape or the form of a butterfly?
How can you share this experience with other people
if they have never seen light? How can you believe
that the reality of sound is the only reality that exists?

Now we can understand why Moses came down
from the mountain and talked about the Promised
Land. What else could he say? Or we can understand what Jesus felt after spending forty days in
the desert, when he talked about the Kingdom of
Heaven. Or when Buddha awoke from under the
bodhi tree and talked about Nirvana. When you

open your spiritual eyes, the first thing you say is "I am with God and the angels. I am in heaven, in paradise, where everything is so beautiful. In the city of God, only beauty and goodness exist; there is no place for fear or suffering. It's just beautiful." People see that you have changed. They see your emotional reaction and know that something profound has happened to you.

From my point of view, the reality I experienced is all of that together; it is ecstasy all the time. In my personal mythology, I experienced the reality of truth, the reality of love. It's a reality that belongs to all of us, but we just don't see it. And if we don't see it, it's because we are blinded by all of the lies from thousands of years ago. If you can open what I call *the spiritual eyes*, you will perceive *what is* without the lies, and I can assure you that your emotional reaction will be overwhelming. For you it is no longer a theory that your story is just a dream. Heaven is the truth, but the story you are perceiving right now is not the truth; it's an illusion.

What is real is so beautiful and there are no words to explain it, but it's there. There is a whole reality created by the reflection of emotions, and in that reality you can see that what is real is your love. I know that I used to perceive that reality before I learned to speak. I know that before the voice of knowledge, all of us perceived that reality all of the time. What you are is something incredibly magnificent. And not just humans, but every animal, every flower, every rock, because everything is the same. When you open your spiritual eyes, you see the simplicity of life. I am life, and you are life. There is no empty space in the universe because everything is full of life. But life is a force that you cannot see. You only see the effects of life, the process of life in action.

You see a flower opening or a tree with the leaves changing colors and falling to the ground. You see a child growing. You see a human becoming old. You have the sense of time, but it's nothing but the reaction of life passing through matter. You don't see yourself, but you see the manifestation of life in your physical body. If you can move your hand, you can see the manifestation of being alive. If you hear your voice, you hear the manifestation of being alive. You see your own physical body when you used to have little hands and very fresh skin, then big hands. You see all these changes in your own physical body, but you still feel that you are the same person.

The closest I can come to describing what you are is that you are a force of life that is transforming everything. This force is moving every atom of your physical body. This force is creating every thought. The spirit of life expresses itself through your physical body, and your physical body can say, "I am alive," because that force of transformation lives in every cell of your physical body. That force has the awareness to perceive an entire reality, that force feels everything. Your physical body is perceiving you right now. Your body can feel you, and when your body feels you, it goes into ecstasy. Your mind can also feel you, and when your mind feels you,

you can experience such intense love and compassion that you don't think any longer.

I see my physical body as a mirror where life, through light, can see itself. I see my physical body as the evolution of life. Life is evolving, it is pushing matter, it is creating. The creation of humanity is not over yet. The creation of humanity is happening right now in your physical body. That force is helping you evolve. That force makes you perceive, analyze, dream, and create a story about everything you perceive.

Life is the force that God uses to create everything at every moment. There is no difference between humans, dogs, cats, trees. Everything is moved by the same force of life. From my point of view, I am that force. Thanks to life, I create my art, I create my whole experience, and it's amazing. Because of me, I have emotions. Because of me, I create knowledge and I can talk. Because of me, I create the story. The force that makes me think and tell my story is the same force that makes you read and understand. There is no difference, and it's happening right now.

I see myself growing older, and I know that some day I will leave this physical body. When I leave this physical body, the body will return to the earth, but life cannot be destroyed. Life is eternal. It was so clear to me when I encountered the truth that life is only one force acting in billions of directions in the creation of the universe. That force never dies. We are life, and life is immortal. We are indestructible, and I think this is very good news.

Once you open your spiritual eyes, you see the dream of your life, you see how much time you waste by playing with petty concerns, by playing with all of that nonsense and meaningless drama. You see how you keep yourself from enjoying a reality of love, a reality of joy.

With your attention focused on what you believe, you cannot perceive this other reality. If your attention is hooked by the voice of knowledge, you only see your knowledge. You only see what you want to see, not what is really there. You only hear what you want to hear, not what is really expressing its love to you. You only relate with what you believe, with what you know, with what you think you are, which means you relate with your story. And you think you are the story, but are you really? You are neither the physical body nor the story. The story is your creation, and, believe it or not, your physical body is also your creation because what you really are is that force of life.

All of us are only one living being, and we come from the same place. There is no difference between any of us; we are the same. You can look at your hand and see that there are five fingers. If you focus your eyes on one finger at a time, you might believe they are different, but it's only one hand. It's the same thing with humanity. There is only one living being, and that being is a force that is moving each of us like a finger on a hand. But all of the fingers belong to one hand. Humans share the same spirit; we share the same soul. There is no difference between me and you — not in my eyes. I know that I am you, and I have no doubt at all because I can see that way.

Behind your story is the real you, and it's full of love. The goodness is right there because what you are is goodness. You don't have to try to be good; you just need to stop pretending to be what you are not. You are one with God, and it is effortless. God is here, and you can feel the presence of God. Of course, if you don't feel God's presence, you need to detach from the story because the only thing between you and God is your story.

Once you find yourself, what you *really* are, you cannot explain what you are because there are no words to explain it. If you use knowledge, you never know what you are, but you know that you are because you exist. You are alive, and you don't need to justify your existence. You can be the biggest mystery in your own story.

POINTS TO PONDER

• There is another reality right here and now, and it is more than the reality of light and sound that we normally perceive. In this reality, we can perceive the reflection of emotions coming from every object. In this reality, what is real is our love.

• The reality of truth, the reality of love, is a reality that belongs to us. Before the voice of knowledge, all of us perceived this reality all of the time. If we don't see it now, it's because we are being blinded by all of the lies from thousands of years ago.

• The energy of love is just like the light that comes from the sun. Like sunlight, the emotion of love looks different depending on what is reflecting the love.

• If you open your spiritual eyes, you perceive *what is* without the lies. For you it is no longer a theory that your story is just a dream. Heaven is the truth, but the story you are perceiving right now is not the truth; it's an illusion.

• Life is a force that you cannot see. You only see the effects of life, the process of life in action. You don't see yourself, but you see the manifestation of life in your physical body. You have the sense of time, but it's nothing but the reaction of life passing through you.

• What you are is something incredibly magnificent. You are life, and not just you, but every animal, every flower, every rock is life, because everything is full of life. All of us are only one living being, and we come from the same place.

12

THE TREE OF LIFE

The story comes full circle

I BELIEVE THAT EVERY HUMAN IS AN ANGEL WITH a message to deliver. I am an angel. Right now I am delivering a message to you. You are also an angel — perhaps you don't know it, but you're still an angel. Humans are always sharing opinions and delivering messages. Is this not true? We can hardly wait for our children to grow up so we can teach them what we know. We want to put all of those seeds in their little heads: what is right, what is wrong; what is good, what is bad. And what is the message that we deliver to our own kids? Do what I say, but not what I do? Tell me the truth when I lie all the time?

There are two kinds of angels: angels who share truth and angels who share lies. The question is: What kind of angels are we? What kind of message do we deliver? When humans lived in Paradise before knowledge, we were angels who shared truth. When we ate the fruit of the Tree of Knowledge and the fallen angel reproduced itself in our mind, we humans also became fallen angels. We are fallen angels because we deliver lies, even if we don't know that we are lying.

The voice of the fallen angel is so loud that we cannot hear the other voice that is silent, what I call *the voice of the spirit*, our *integrity, the voice of love.* This silent voice is always there. Before we learned to speak, when we were one and two years old, we listened to this voice.

When I was a child, I used to watch Walt Disney's Donald Duck cartoons. On one side of Donald Duck's head was an angel, and on the other side of his head was a devil, and both were talking to him. Well, this is real. The storyteller is that little devil. You have a voice that is telling you why you are not good enough, why you don't deserve love, why you cannot trust, why you will never be great or beautiful or perfect. That voice is lying, and the only power that it has is the power that you give it.

The voice of knowledge is loud; it's not silent. The voice of your spirit is silent because it doesn't need to talk to you. Your body doesn't need to know how to be perfect from your point of view because it *is* perfect. When you are born, you don't know what you are, not with words. But your body knows what it is, and it doesn't need to explain it with words, just as your liver doesn't need to go to medical school to function with the rest of your body. It just knows what to do.

There are other things that you just know. If you are a woman, you don't need to learn how to be a woman; you don't need to learn how to develop a fetus or how to deliver a baby. Just by nature, you are what you are; you don't need to learn to be what you are. This is silent knowledge. You just know. You can feel silent knowledge when you close your eyes. You can feel silent knowledge every time you breathe.

You are an angel, and your life is your message. But what kind of angel do you want to be? You cannot serve two masters. You cannot share lies and share truth at the same time. Doesn't that make sense?

Knowledge used to be the greatest tyrant in my life. I used to be a slave of knowledge, but knowledge no longer has power over me. And it doesn't have power over me because I no longer believe knowledge. I no longer accept that voice in my head telling me why nobody likes me, why I'm not worth it, why I'm not perfect. Now knowledge is just a tool of communication in my pocket. What I know is wonderful because, thanks to knowledge, I can talk to you and you can understand me. That is what I am doing right now — communicating through knowledge. Everything I'm telling you is the expression of my art. In the same way that Picasso uses color to make a portrait, I use knowledge to make a portrait of what I see and feel.

Three or four thousand years ago, humans discovered that knowledge is contaminated by lies. If we clean all of the lies from our knowledge, we will go back to the paradise that we lost. We will return to truth, return to love, and reunite with God. Now we can see that the story of Adam and Eve is not just a fable, but a symbol that was created by a master who discovered the same thing that the Toltec discovered. The creator of this story obviously knew the truth, and the symbolism is so beautiful.

Yes, the fallen angel who lived in the original Tree of Knowledge was reproduced in every human and it's controlling people's lives even now. We are possessed, but there's no reason to be afraid. The big demon is merely a lie, and its lies haven't destroyed us yet. They have done their best, but they have failed because we are more powerful than that fallen angel. We are only one living being, and we have been living in this world for thousands of years.

Adam and Eve didn't die. They are here because we are here. You are Adam, and you are Eve. And we are trying so hard to go back to the place we came from — Paradise, that place of love and truth. You know that it's there because you have it in your memory. You were there when you were born, and during the first and second years of your life, you were physically there.

Prophecies from many different philosophies of the world tell us that we are going back to that place of love. Some call it the Kingdom of Heaven; others call it Nirvana or the Promised Land. The Toltec call it the Dream of the Second Attention. Every philosophy has a different name, but the meaning is the same: It is a place of joy and love. It is a place of unity, the unity of all our hearts. It is the reunion with life because we are the manifestation of the one living being that exists.

The Toltec believe that one day common sense will rule the dream of humanity. When that happens, we will discover that everything, and everybody, is perfect. It will take time to fulfill the dreams of these prophets who knew what would happen. When they talked about a society of love and happiness, it's because they lived their lives in that way, and they knew that we are all the same. If one person can reach a place like that, everybody can do it. There are also prophets who talk about destruction and fear, but I believe that we, the humans, are evolving in the right direction. The only problem is that there are billions of us, and in order for the entire society to change, there has to be a great effort. But it's not impossible.

Everything can change, and everything will change. It just takes time. In the last century, we have witnessed rapid changes in science and technology. Psychology has stayed a little behind, but it will catch up. The world in our present-day society is completely different from the society we lived in forty or fifty years ago. There are fewer lies today than there were eight hundred years ago. Just by seeing our evolution, I have faith that we will recover paradise.

Just imagine waking up and finding yourself in Europe during the Middle Ages. You see people suffering because their lives are ruled by superstition; they live in constant fear because of the lies they believe. Do you think you could live your life the way you are living it now? I don't think so. Imagine that you are a woman wanting to tell everybody about the beliefs that rule your life right now. You can see that you don't fit in their dream. For you, their dream is a real nightmare. You want to tell the women that they don't need to suffer anymore, that they don't need to be abused. You want to tell them that they are humans, too, that they have a soul, that they have the right to be happy, that they have the right to express themselves in life.

How do you think everybody will judge you if you take these ideas to them? Surely they will say that you are evil, that you are possessed, that the devil is speaking through your mouth. How long do you think you would survive? Yes, not long, because they would burn you alive. If you think that our present society is hell, that society really was hell. For us, it is obvious that the social, moral, and religious rules of that time were based on lies, but for them it was not that obvious.

Perhaps the lies you believe about yourself are not so obvious to you, but you can see the result of what you believe. And what is the result? Well, how you live your life. When you believe the truth, the result is happiness, love, goodness. You feel good about yourself and you feel good about everything. If you are not happy, it's because you believe in lies. That is the origin of all human conflict. All of our suffering comes from believing in lies.

How can we stop all the human injustice, all the war, all the destruction of our Mother Earth? Well, by not believing in lies. It sounds very simple, but you can just imagine how complicated it is to rearrange the belief system of an entire country or all of humanity. Humans don't want their lies to be challenged because they are not in control of their mind. Who is controlling the human mind? Lies have total control of humanity. This is what you learn in any mystery school when you reach a certain level of preparation. It is something so simple, yet it is one of the highest revelations in any mystery school.

The real enemy is lies, and this used to be top secret in most traditions because people believed that whoever knew this would have power over other people, and they might misuse the power. That was the excuse, but I think that those who understood the truth were probably afraid to share it. Why? Because the people who believed in lies would be frightened of the truth and burn them alive. In fact, that is what happened in many parts of the world.

Then how will we recover the paradise we lost? The solution is simple: The truth will set us free. That is the whole key to going back to heaven.

When you recover the truth, *your* truth, a miracle happens. You open your spiritual eyes and return to heaven. Heaven is the most beautiful story made with love, and guess who creates heaven? We create our own heaven. Heaven is a story; it is a dream that we, as life, can create. But for life to create heaven, the main character of the story needs to surrender to life, and allow life to manifest without the lies.

Heaven is here, and it's available for everybody. Paradise is here, but we need to have the eyes to perceive it. This is exactly what Jesus and Buddha and Moses and Krishna promised so long ago, and all of the great masters in the world who created heaven in their own mind. They are all telling you that it's up to you. If they can do it, you can do it, and if you can do it, everybody can do it.

The truth will set us free, but lies keep us in this reality. I don't know how long ago humans first understood this, but it's so simple that nobody wants to understand it. They want something more complicated than this because the storyteller works that way. If we don't believe in lies, we are already in the healing process. The Christian Mystery School knew this, the Egyptians knew this, and the Toltec knew this, but it was difficult to put it into words. Then they created legends such as the story of Adam and Eve.

And that reminds me of the other half of the story of Adam and Eve. In Paradise, there is another tree, and it is the Tree of Life, or the Tree of Truth. The legend says that whoever eats the fruit of the Tree of Life, which is truth, will live forever in Paradise because life is the eternal truth. The fruit of the Tree of Life is the message that comes directly from life or from God. Life is the only truth; it is the force that is creating all of the time. When you see that force in yourself, and when you put your faith in that force, you are truly alive.

Now we can understand what Jesus meant when he said, "I am life, and only through me can you reach heaven." He was not talking about the person Jesus; he was talking about being the Tree of Life.

What he was trying to say is: "I am the Tree of Life. Whoever eats my fruit will live with me in the kingdom of heaven. The kingdom of heaven is a kingdom where everybody is a king."

Isn't this the same thing we are saying here? You are the king in your own reality; you are responsible for your own dream of life. Jesus also said, "The kingdom of heaven is just like a wedding where you are the bride, and truth or God is the groom, and you live in an eternal honeymoon." Isn't that beautiful?

The truth cannot be explained with words, so Jesus tried to use a concept that everybody could understand. He compared the reality that we spoke of before to a honeymoon. When you are married to the truth, you live in an eternal honeymoon. In the honeymoon, everything in your life is about love. When you are in love, you see everything with the eyes of love. When you are making love all the time, everything is wonderful and beautiful, and you can grasp heaven.

Now we can understand what Jesus meant when he spoke about forgiveness, about love, about heaven. He said, "Let the children come with me because the ones who are like them can enter the kingdom of heaven." When you are a child before you have knowledge, which means before you eat all of the lies, you live in heaven. When you fall, it is because you are innocent. And when you recover that paradise, you become like a child again, but with a big difference. Now you are no longer innocent; you are wise. This gives you immunity; you cannot fall again.

We can also say that you become wise when you finally eat the fruit of the Tree of Life. To eat the fruit of this tree is symbolic of illumination. Illumination is when you become light, but there are no words to describe this experience. That is why we have to use mythology and our imagination to grasp what it means. To really know what it is, we need to experience it, to be there. The truth is the real you; it's your own integrity. Nobody can guide you to that place. Only you can take yourself there.

You can change your own story, but it begins with you, the main character of your story. You can transform yourself from a messenger of lies, fear, and destruction to a messenger of truth, love, and creation. When you return to the truth, the way you express yourself in society is much better. Your communication improves. Your creation is stronger and more powerful. In all directions, life as you know it changes for the better.

You don't need to change the world; you need to change yourself. And you have to do it in your own way because only you have the possibility of knowing yourself. It's obvious that you cannot change the world, at least not yet, because the world is not prepared for the truth. You can only change yourself, but that is a big step. By returning to the truth, you take a big step for everybody else.

The gates of heaven are open, and heaven is waiting for you. But if you don't enter heaven, it's because you believe that you are not worthy of heaven. You believe that you are not worthy of living in a place of truth, joy, and love. This is a lie, but if you believe it, that lie controls your story, and you cannot pass through the gates of heaven.

The truth is not in the story. The truth is in the power that creates the story. That power is life; it is God. I discovered this long ago, and my hope is that you can understand what I am saying. To really understand, it's not enough for your reasoning mind to say, "Oh yes, it's true, it's logical." No, you need to understand with your heart. I really wish that you would take this into your heart because it can change your whole life. Don't believe me with your head, but feel what I am saying with your heart. Focus your attention on what you feel, and what you will perceive is your own integrity speaking to you. What is truth is truth, and a very powerful part of you can recognize truth. Believe your heart.

Your life will become a masterpiece of art when the storyteller finally tells you only truth. When the voice of knowledge becomes the voice of integrity, you return to the truth, you return to heaven, you return to love, and the cycle is over. When this happens, you no longer believe your own storyteller or anybody else's storyteller. This is my story, and you don't have to believe my story either. It's up to you to believe it or not, but this is the way that I see the world.

The moment when I perceived the infinite, I saw that there is only one living being in the universe. That one living being is God, and because everything and everybody is a manifestation of that one living being, everything and everybody will return to that source.

There is nothing to fear anymore; we don't have to be afraid to die. There is only one force that exists, and when we die, everybody is going back to the same place. Even if we don't want to, even if we resist, we will return to that place because there is no other place to go. This is the greatest news for everybody. There's no need to be afraid that we will be condemned when we die. In the moment of our death, I am going back to God, you are going back to God, everybody is going back to God, and that's it.

And it's not about being good enough for God. God doesn't care if we are good enough. God just loves us.

Our life is a story; our life is a dream. The kingdom of heaven is in our mind, and it's just a choice to return to our authentic self, to live our life in love and in truth. There is no reason for our life to be controlled by fear and lies. If we recover the control of our story, that gives us the freedom to create our life as beautifully as we can, as an artist of the spirit. Once we know that everybody is returning to God, which is truth, then believing in lies is just nonsense. The lies in our story are not important. What is important is to enjoy our time in this reality, to live in happiness while we are alive.

The question is: What are you going to do with your story? My choice is to write my story with truth and with love. What is yours?

Points to Ponder

• The voice of the fallen angel is so loud that we cannot hear the voice of our spirit, our integrity, our love. This silent voice is always there. Before we learned to speak, when we were one and two years old, we listened to this voice.

• When you are born, you don't know what you are, but your body knows what it is, and it knows what to do. This is silent knowledge. You can feel silent knowledge every time you breathe.

• You are an angel, and your life is your message. You can be a messenger of lies, fear, and destruction, or a messenger of truth, love, and creation. But you cannot deliver lies and truth at the same time.

• Heaven is a story that we can create when we surrender to life and allow life to manifest without lies. Heaven is here, and it's available for everybody, but we need to have the eyes to perceive it.

• The fruit of the Tree of Life is life; it is truth. Life is the only truth; it is the force that is creating all the time. When you see this force in yourself, and you put your faith in this force, you are truly alive.

• The truth is not in the story. The truth is in the power that creates the story. The truth is the real you; it's your own integrity, and nobody can guide you to that place. Only you can take yourself there.

• When the voice of knowledge becomes the voice of integrity, you return to the truth, you return to love, you return to heaven, and live in happiness again.

Prayers

PLEASE TAKE A MOMENT TO CLOSE YOUR EYES, OPEN your heart, and feel the love that is all around you. I invite you to join me in a special prayer to experience a communion with our Creator.

Focus your attention on your lungs, as if only your lungs exist. Take a deep breath and feel the air as it fills your lungs. Notice the connection of love between the air and your lungs. Feel the pleasure when your lungs expand to fulfill the biggest need of the human body — to breathe. Take another deep breath, then exhale and feel the pleasure again.

Just to breathe is enough for us to always enjoy life. Feel the pleasure of being alive, the pleasure of the feeling of love. . . .

PRAYER FOR THE CREATOR

Today, Creator, help me to create the story of my life as beautifully as you create the entire universe.

Beginning today, help me to recover my faith in the truth, in the silent voice of my integrity. I ask you, God, to manifest your love through me in every word I express, in every action I take. Help me to make every activity in my life a ritual of love and joy. Let me use love as the material for creating the most beautiful story about your creation.

Today, God, my heart is filled with gratitude for the gift of life. Thank you for the awareness that you only create perfection, and because you created me, I believe in my own perfection.

God, help me to love myself unconditionally so that I can share my love with other humans, with all forms of life on this beautiful planet. Help me to create my own dream of heaven, to the eternal happiness of humanity. Amen.

PRAYER FOR AN ANGEL

Today, Creator, help me to remember my real nature, which is love and happiness. Help me to become what I really am, and to express what I really am.

Beginning today, help me to recognize every human as your messenger with a message to deliver. Help me to see you in the soul of every human, behind the masks, behind the images we pretend to be. Today, help me to deliver the message of my integrity to that part of me that is always judging. Help me, God, to let go of all my judgments, to let go of all the false messages I deliver to myself and to everyone around me.

Today, help me to recover the awareness of my own creation as an angel, and let me use my awareness to deliver your message of life, your message of joy, your message of love. Let me express the beauty of my spirit, the beauty of my heart, in the supreme art of humans: the dream of my life. Amen.

About the Authors

Don miguel ruiz is a master of the toltec mystery school tradition. For more than two decades, he has worked to impart the wisdom of the ancient Toltec to a small group of students and apprentices, guiding them toward their personal freedom. Today, he continues to combine his unique blend of ancient wisdom and modern-day awareness through lectures, workshops, and journeys to sacred sites around the world.

For information about current programs offered by don Miguel Ruiz and his apprentices, please visit his website: www.miguelruiz.com

Janet mills is the editor and publisher of amber-allen Publishing. She is the author of *The Power of a Woman* and *Free of Dieting Forever*, and the editor of *The Seven Spiritual Laws of Success* by Deepak Chopra, an international bestseller with over two million copies in print. Her life's mission is to publish books of enduring beauty, integrity, and wisdom, and to inspire others to fulfill their most cherished dreams.

*Prayers: A Communion with our Creator**

A beautiful collection of don Miguel's prayers (including the popular *Circle of Fire* prayer), guided meditations, and powerful prose that will inspire and transform your life.

The Voice of Knowledge Audiobook

In this abridged reading of *The Voice of Knowledge*, actor Peter Coyote brings to life don Miguel's profound teachings.

Toltec Wisdom Card Decks

Each card deck contains 48 beautifully illustrated cards with pearls of wisdom from *The Four Agreements*, *The Mastery of Love*, and *The Voice of Knowledge*.

❧

For a free catalog of Amber-Allen titles, call or write:

Amber-Allen Publishing
Post Office Box 6657
San Rafael, California 94903-0657
(800) 624-8855

Visit us online: www.amberallen.com

**Also available in Spanish*